Access to Information

A Review of the Provision of Disability Information

Nick Moore

POLICY STUDIES INSTITUTE
London

The publishing imprint of the independent
POLICY STUDIES INSTITUTE
100 Park Village East, London NW1 3SR
Telephone: 0171-387 2171   Fax: 0171-388 0914

© Policy Studies Institute 1995

ISBN 0 85374 663 X

PSI Research Report 765

A CIP catalogue record of this book is available from the British Library.

1 2 3 4 5 6 7 8 9

PSI publications are available from
BEBC Distribution Ltd
P O Box 1496, Poole, Dorset, BH12 3YD

Books will normally be despatched within 24 hours. Cheques should be made payable
to BEBC Distribution Ltd.

Credit card and telephone/fax orders may be placed on the following freephone
numbers:

FREEPHONE: 0800 262260
FREEFAX: 0800 262266

Booktrade representation (UK & Eire):
Broadcast Books
24 De Montfort Road, London SW16 1LW
Telephone: 0181-677 5129

PSI subscriptions are available from PSI's subscription agent
Carfax Publishing Company Ltd
P O Box 25, Abingdon, Oxford OX14 3UE

Laserset by Policy Studies Institute
Printed in Great Britain by Redwood Books, Trowbridge, Wiltshire

This book is dedicated to
Laura Cale

Contents

Acknowledgements

Many people have contributed to the National Disability Information Project. I would like to acknowledge the work of all those associated with the 12 pilot projects – both the paid and volunteer staff and the members of the management committees. They achieved a great deal. Also, many people working in the national information providers supported the aims of NDIP and worked hard to achieve them. It is particularly gratifying to see representatives of both national and local services working together to establish an new organisation that can take over now that NDIP has come to an end.

The role of the Department of Health needs special mention. The Department did much more than provide the money. Its early commitment to the project, expressed through the efforts of Una O'Brien and Siân Thomas, provided a much-needed initial impetus. NDIP continued to benefit greatly by the constructive support and advice that was offered by Glynis Phillips and her team: Warren Brown, Margaret Lowry and Ted Webb.

Many other people contributed support and encouragement along the way. I would like to acknowledge the particular contribution made by Dot McGahan and Hugh Lyon of DIAL UK; by Colin Barnes of the Disability Research Unit at Leeds University; by Martin Jones and Jan Tallis of the Computer Development Unit at the London Advice Services Alliance; by Marion Fitzpatrick, Caroline Boswell and Margie Butler of the Consultancy, Information and Policy Unit of LASA; by Clare Nankivell of the University of Central England and by Naomi Gould and her team at the Disability Information Service in Surrey.

At the Policy Studies Institute I was fortunate to be supported by a team of very able individuals: Philipa Hinkley, Pamela Nadash, Michael Rooney, Michael Shiner and Rebecca Simpkins all served as project officers at different stages; Sue Johnson, the Institute Librarian, provided her usual high level of support and kept the pilot projects abreast of developments through the *Current Awareness Bulletin*; Sarah Waterton and Amanda Trafford dealt with the large volume of administrative work that a project like this generates, while the indefatigable Sara Mason kept us all on our toes.

None of this, however, would have come to anything without the calm and utterly reliable work carried out by Jane Steele. She undertook the day-to-day management of the Project Team and deserves the full credit for its achievements.

Finally, a number of people have read all or part of this report in draft. Representatives of the pilot projects have offered valuable comments on Chapter 5 and Gerry Zarb provided useful comments on Chapter 2. Bob Gann, Sue Johnson, Sara Mason, Glynis Phillips and Jane Steele have read the full report in draft and have made many comments and suggestions that have improved the text. To them I express my thanks while accepting full responsibility for any remaining inaccuracies or deficiencies. The opinions and conclusions expressed in this final draft are mine alone. I hope that I have been able to do justice to the work of so many people.

Nick Moore
February 1995

Part I

The origins of the National Disability Information Project

The National Disability Information Project ran for three years from the autumn of 1991. As a piece of social engineering, it is typical of the approach adopted by the British government in the late twentieth century.

The government, having used independent management consultants to define the problem and to identify possible solutions, established a project that would enable these solutions to be demonstrated in the expectation that others would perceive the value of the activity and would carry on the good work. The government acted as an enabler, with a clearly defined brief and a time-limited responsibility for funding.

As such, NDIP, as the National Disability Information Project became known, is no different from many of the projects that have been launched in recent years. The origins of the project, however, can be traced back well before the 1990s. The conditions that brought NDIP into being were the product of three separate but related developments: the growth of advice services; the moves towards equal opportunities for disabled people; and a new interpretation of the concept of citizenship.

To understand NDIP and to evaluate its achievements, or otherwise, it is necessary to begin by understanding the dynamics of the social forces that gave the project shape.

Part I   Contents

1   The development of advice services

Britain, like many other advanced social democracies, has a network of locally based agencies that exist to meet a general need for information and advice about the workings of the welfare state.

The need for these services has long been recognised. William Beveridge in his report on social security included a recommendation that 'there should be in every local Security Office an advice bureau to which every person in doubt or difficulty can be referred' (Beveridge, 1942).

In Britain, despite Beveridge's recommendation, the services have actually developed within the voluntary sector and, despite being funded by local authorities and other statutory bodies, they are independent of the main service providers. This independence is perceived to be one of their greatest strengths.

Advice services act on behalf of their clients. They are not simply channels that service providers and others can use to communicate with the public. Rather, they are advisers and advocates to whom people can turn in much the same way that others might turn to solicitors or accountants.

Increasingly service providers recognise that advice services have an important role to play in ensuring that our complex social welfare system operates effectively. It has, however, taken some time for this recognition to develop – on a number of occasions, advice services have faced thinly disguised hostility. This is surprising, given the origins of the service.

Early origins
The need for public information and advice service predates Beveridge and his report. As the welfare state began to emerge after the First World War it became apparent that people needed a considerable amount of information if they were to be able to take advantage of the services that were being provided for them. At the same time, people needed to be well-informed to understand the complexities of a system with limited resources and an often complex set of entitlements.

It took the prospect of the Second World War to translate this general perception of information and advice as a corollary of the welfare state into actual services. In 1938 the National Council of Social Services drew up a plan for the development of a national network of local advice services. The plan was put into effect on the outbreak of war and by October 1939 over 200 citizens advice bureaux had been created. By 1943 the number had risen to 1,060 (Citron, 1989).

Two characteristics of advice services were defined at this early stage. First the services were part of the voluntary sector. Secondly, each service was independent and governed by a management committee that broadly represented the service's users.

It is interesting to note that the Ministry of Health accepted the responsibility for funding the citizens advice bureaux and a central servicing office within the National Council of Social Services. After the war, central government passed the responsibility for funding to local authorities – a shift that had the effect of reducing the number of services to 416 in 1960. The bureaux each contributed to the cost of the central office, confirming a third characteristic of advice services – that there are distinct advantages in providing some support services from a central base.

During the post-war period a fourth characteristic became established – advice services were seen to have an important role in feeding back to government information about the consequences of social legislation.

The citizens advice bureaux service became more firmly established during the 1960s. Central government resumed responsibility for funding the central office: the Ministry of Health provided a series of grants in recognition of the increased demand on services arising from its housing legislation; the Board of Trade provided funds in recognition of the service's advice work with consumers and other contributions were made by the Home Office and the Civil Service Department.

In the late 1960s the establishment overtones of the CAB service were increasingly called into question. A much more radical form of service was being developed as part of the experimental, government-funded Community Development Projects. These were locally based attempts to overcome deprivation and disadvantage. They adopted a number of strategies, many of which involved some form of advice work. But this was advice work rooted in community activism and was a far cry from the middle-class associations of many CABx. It spawned two types of advice services that have since had a significant impact on the overall pattern of provision – law centres and independent neighbourhood advice centres.

A number of legal advice centres had been established during the 1960s. These were mostly voluntary associations of solicitors offering advice sessions in their spare time. Some services were operated in conjunction with the local CAB. Such services were not often available in areas of greatest deprivation and the community development projects served to demonstrate their lack and the limitations of a service offering little more than advice and referral to a solicitor.

The first law centre was established in North Kensington in 1970. The defining characteristic of law centres was that they were able to take on cases on behalf of clients. They offered legal advice and assistance free at the point of use. Where appropriate they referred people on to local solicitors but they took up the more pressing cases themselves. They employed qualified solicitors and received funds from the Lord Chancellor's Department, from fees for legal aid work and, in some cases, from local authorities.

Independent neighbourhood advice centres were also established as community based projects in which advice provision was seen as part of an overall attempt to overcome social deprivation. The use of the term 'independent' was often part of a deliberate attempt to distance the centres from the citizens advice bureau service.

By the end of the 1960s it was possible to determine the beginnings of a national network of advice services ranging from the citizens advice bureaux on one hand to the more radical law centres and independent advice centres on the other.

Steady growth

The network grew steadily during the 1970s. The citizens advice bureau service attracted more stable funding from central government (channelled through a surprising array of different departments), supplemented by occasional but substantial development grants. The number of bureaux grew from about 500 at the beginning of the decade to well over 800 at the end. Together they dealt with over 3.5 million enquiries each year (Citron, 1989).

The network of law centres grew from one in 1970 to 42 in the early 1980s (National Consumer Council, 1983). They joined together to form the Law Centres Federation and this central body was supported by funds from the Lord Chancellor's Department.

Independent neighbourhood advice centres also grew in number. Given the nature of these intensely local services, it is difficult to know how many are in existence at any one time. By the early 1980s, however, they had established the Federation of Independent Advice Centres (FIAC) to represent their interests. Over 50 centres were in direct membership of

FIAC at the time of the NCC report but three or four times that number were thought to exist.

Services were developed to meet the need for consumer and housing advice. Consumer advice centres were supported during the 1970s by a central government grant to local authorities. Under this arrangement 126 such centres were operating in 1979.

Housing advice centres were first recommended by the Seebohm report on social services in 1968 (Committee on Local Authority and Allied Personal Social Services, 1968). The first two were opened in London in 1969 and by the end of the 1970s there were more than 150 of them. Two-thirds of these were part of local authority housing departments, dealing mainly with council housing problems. The remaining third were independent and dealt mainly with the private sector.

The 1970s saw the emergence of two other types of advice service. These were not focused on a particular community or on a specific subject area. Instead they sought to meet the needs of a particular group of people within the local community. In the middle of the 1970s a number of telephone-based advice services for disabled people were established. At about the same time a number of services were established to provide advice for young people.

The Disablement Information and Advice Line (DIAL) services were one of a number of services that developed from the Independent Living movement in Derbyshire. They sought to specialise in advice about the problems faced by disabled people. They were controlled and staffed by people with personal experience of disability and made extensive use of telephones to overcome problems of access.

In 1977 the then existing DIALs came together to form DIAL UK to provide common services and to represent the local interests at national level. By the early 1980s the number of DIALs had grown to 54 (National Consumer Council, 1983).

Counselling and advisory services for young people grew in number during the 1970s and by 1983 there were 75 services in existence, 59 of which were members of the National Association of Counselling and Young People's Advisory Services (NAYPCAS).

The logical justification for the development of this network of advice centres was provided by the National Consumer Council in its seminal report *The fourth right of citizenship,* published in 1976. This documented the development and scale of the provision of advice services and traced their origins back to Beveridge and to TH Marshall's concept of citizenship (Marshall, 1950). Marshall identified three sets of rights. The first are civil rights: the right to liberty of the person; to freedom of speech, thought and faith and the right to justice. The second set of rights are political rights: to vote for local and central government. Third are the social rights – what Beveridge defined as 'the right to a minimum standard of life below which [the citizen] should not be allowed to fall'. The NCC argued that these three sets of rights were meaningless without a fourth – the right to information. They argued that:

> People will not be able to get their due as citizens of present day society unless they have continuous access to the information that will guide them through it and, where necessary, the advice to help them translate that information into effective action: and unless they get their due they are unlikely to recognise the reciprocal obligation that all citizens have to society (National Consumer Council, 1977).

Threats and uncertainty

The optimism and expansion of the 1970s gave way to uncertainty and instability. There followed a period when the consensus about the value of advice services was threatened.

The early 1980s was a time of severe financial restraint. In an attempt to exert control over public expenditure, central government cut or reduced expenditure on what were regarded as non-essential items. Local authority budgets were similarly squeezed. The impact on advice services was severe.

An early casualty was the network of consumer advice services that had been supported by a central government grant to local authorities. The grant was abolished in 1980 and the number of services dropped from 126 to 58, many of those remaining being reduced in scale and absorbed into the local authority trading standards departments. Central government support for housing advice was also reduced substantially over this period.

Other networks survived better. The law centres movement suffered some setbacks with reductions in funding in some local authority areas and increased uncertainty about support from the Lord Chancellor's Department. Independent advice centres suffered through cutbacks in local authority support and through a steady erosion of local funding made available by the Department of the Environment through the succession of Urban Aid, Urban Programme and now City Challenge programmes.

The financial pressures slowed the development of DIALs and youth advice services. The number of DIALs grew slowly from under 50 to nearly 80.

The citizens advice bureaux network struggled financially but faced a threat that was potentially more damaging. In 1983 Dr Gerard Vaughan, the then Minister of State for Consumer Affairs and controller of the grant to the National Association of Citizens Advice Bureaux (NACAB) became concerned about political bias within the service. The deputy manager of the CAB in Reading – Joan Ruddock, who went on to become a Member of Parliament – was appointed to chair the Campaign for Nuclear Disarmament. The appointment came at a time when the government was particularly sensitive to nuclear campaigners and Dr Vaughan raised a question about the impartiality of the service .

The government made only a temporary grant to NACAB pending a full review. This was carried out by Sir Douglas Lovelock who reported in 1984.

The Lovelock report exonerated the CAB service in these words:

> The Citizens Advice Bureaux service is an invaluable national asset. The provision of a service of information, advice and guidance meets a real and growing need. The dedication and competence of the service have earned widespread respect. Because the service's standards are high and because it relies predominantly on a volunteer workforce, it represents extraordinarily good value for money. (Lovelock, 1984)

This proved to be a very important endorsement, not only of the CAB service, but of advice services generally. The Lovelock report was well-received in all political parties and since then advice services have ceased to be a matter over which there is serious political contention.

Other developments in the late 1970s and early 1980s had served to consolidate the networks of advice services. In 1978 the Community Information Project was established with funding from the British Library. The Project worked to codify and disseminate much of the experience that had been gained by local advice services. They also helped to foster the emerging networks, in particular DIAL UK and FIAC (Community Information Project, 1982).

In 1979, along with the National Consumer Council, the Community Information Project established a working party of all the advice service networks to combat the looming financial crisis for advice services. From this working party developed the Advice Services Alliance that has, since that time, met regularly to coordinate the planning and development of advice services.

This collaboration produced more than an effective political lobby. A series of publications provided practical help to the networks and to local groups. *Know how* (Morby, 1982) was a guide to publications and other information that could be used by advice centres. *Good advice for all* (National Consumer Council, 1986) set out the basic resource standards that were required by advice services. *Going for advice* (Advice Services Alliance, 1987) provided guidance on preparing local development plans for advice services. All this helped to strengthen local services and to foster a spirit of cooperation and coordinated service planning at both national and local level.

General acceptance

The need for effective advice services is now generally accepted. They are no longer the subject of political contention at national level. Within many local authorities they have become accepted as part of the local pattern of services. And most of the key executive agencies have accepted that advice services play an important role in ensuring that the social welfare system operates effectively. The Benefits Agency, in particular, acknowledges in its customer charter that it has a symbiotic relationship with local advice services.

That is not to say that the network of provision is adequate for the needs placed upon it. There is a generally low level of financial support for the services. For example, the average grant received by DIAL services from their local authorities is still only £13,500. And very many advice services in urban areas have to operate with severely restricted opening hours as a means of rationing the demand. It seems inevitable that we will have to await a significant improvement in our national economic performance before financial support is such that the supply of advice services meets the demand for them.

Despite this, the advice services of the early 1990s are incomparably stronger than those of the early 1970s. The services are better resourced and better staffed. The CAB service, for example, decided in the early 1980s to move to a position where every bureau was managed by at least one paid member of staff. The services are better planned and managed. Many local authority areas have undertaken extensive exercises in consultation with local advice agencies to plan the development of advice services. The managers of most services now operate in more sophisticated ways. This is, in part, a reflection of the changes that have taken place within the whole voluntary sector over the last 20 years.

This process of development has served to reinforce the primary characteristics of advice services in Britain. They are *part of the voluntary sector*. As such they are separate from the providers of services and are thus able to act impartially but on behalf of their client. The services are *independent and locally managed* with a high level of perceived *accountability to the service's users*. This independence and accountability is usually achieved by means of a management committee formed from local people.

They are *free at the point of use*. They are funded by government – national or local – and as such there are no charges to limit access to the service. Local services have identified the need for some *national support services* and have organised themselves into *networks* to facilitate this. These networks provide direct services to their local members – information and training services are the most common – and a means of *feeding information back to government on the consequences of their policies*. The networks also provide a means whereby the *local services can have a voice at a national level*.

Britain's network of advice services provides ordinary people with a source of information, advice and help that can be called upon in time of need. The network is not perfect – it is far from being adequately financed – but it is a valuable resource. The National Disability Information Project offered the potential to strengthen the capacity of that network to provide the information, advice and help that disabled people need to cope with the particular problems that society presents them.

References

Advice Services Alliance (1987) *Going for advice: a manual for preparing local development plans for advice services*

Beveridge, William (1942) *Social insurance and allied services* Cmnd 6404. HMSO

Citron, Judith (1989) *The citizens advice bureaux: for the community by the community*. Pluto Press

Committee on Local Authority and Allied Personal Social Services (1968) *Report* (The Seebohm Report). HMSO

Community Information Project (1982) *The first five years*

Lovelock, Sir Douglas (Chairman) (1984) *Review of the National Association of Citizens Advice Bureaux* Cmnd 9139. HMSO

Marshall, TH (1950) *Citizenship and social class*. Cambridge University Press

Morby, Grainne (1982) *Know how to find out your rights*. Pluto Press

National Consumer Council (1977) *The fourth right of citizenship: a review of local advice services*

National Consumer Council (1983) *Information and advice services in the United Kingdom: report to the Minister of State for Consumer Affairs*

National Consumer Council (1986) *Good advice for all: guidelines on standards for local advice services*

2   Equal opportunities for disabled people

For many years services for disabled people in Britain have been based on an individual or medical model of disability. Disability is thought of as something that is personal to the individual – an inability to perform normal activities resulting from an impairment of the body or the mind. Viewed from this perspective, disability is perceived as something that is abnormal – a personal tragedy. More particularly, it is seen as something that can tackled either by attempting to cure or alleviate the effects of the impairment or, if that is not possible, by providing institutional or community care.

Increasingly, that model of disability has been rejected. A better way of understanding disability, it has been argued, is to see it as the outcome of the interaction between a person's physical mental or sensory impairment and the way in which the social environment is constructed. Viewed in this way, disability arises from the barriers that are constructed by society. The responsibility for overcoming disability thus shifts from the individual to society as a whole.

The development of this social model of disability has been part of a growing awareness of disability as a political issue. A product of this has been the steadily increasing pressure for civil rights for disabled people. 'Disabled people have identified institutional discrimination as the main problem and anti-discrimination legislation as the most promising way of tackling it' (Oliver and Barnes, 1991). It is not possible to understand many of the issues raised by the National Disability Information Project without considering them in this shifting political context.

Challenging discrimination

The first piece of British legislation concerned directly with disabled people was the *Disabled Persons (Employment) Act 1944*. This attempted to improve the employment conditions of disabled people but it did so not by giving disabled people any rights to employment. Rather, it imposed duties on employers and others. Employers were required to employ a quota of disabled people and government was required to compile a register of

11

disabled people. The government also took steps to set up sheltered employment schemes.

The Act was a significant step forward, and its basic provisions are still in place. It was, however, firmly rooted in the individual model of disability and attempted to solve the problem by placing duties on organisations rather than giving rights to individuals.

Two other pieces of similar legislation followed: the *Education Act 1944* led to the development of special schooling for disabled children, while the *National Assistance Act 1948* placed duties on local authorities to 'arrange services' for the benefit of disabled people.

The local authority responsibilities were extended by the *Chronically Sick and Disabled Persons Act 1970* which, in addition to requiring local authorities to provide services to those assessed as needing them, imposed a duty to compile a register of disabled people and to inform individuals about services that were known to the authority. The Act was found to be seriously lacking, not least because local authorities gave it a very low priority (Cook and Mitchell, 1982).

So, at the beginning of the 1970s, disabled people were recipients of services made available to them by local authorities and others. They had, however, few rights *as disabled people* and, generally experienced higher than average levels of unemployment and lower than average incomes.

Attitudes towards discrimination, however, were changing. There was sustained pressure to outlaw discrimination on grounds of race and sex. This led to the *Sex Discrimination Act 1975* and the *Race Relations Act 1976*.

From the outset, it was clear that legislation alone would not change attitudes or practice. To help bring about the change the Equal Opportunities Commission and the Commission on Racial Equality were established to promote awareness, to bring test cases and to provide general assistance to individuals and groups who felt that they had been discriminated against. Twenty years later the process continues. There have, however, been discernible changes in attitudes and in the practices and procedures of organisations of all kinds.

The erosion of discrimination on racial and sexual grounds contrasts with the lack of change for disabled people. The situation at the end of the 1970s was documented by two significant reports. In 1979 the Silver Jubilee Access Committee drew attention to the incidence of discrimination against disabled people. The position was confirmed by an official committee set up to investigate the allegations. This found that discrimination was commonplace and recommended anti-discrimination legislation (Committee on Restrictions Against Disabled People, 1982).

The general level of disadvantage experienced by disabled people was confirmed by a series of related studies carried out by the Office of Population Censuses and Surveys in 1985 and 1986 and published in 1988 and 1989. These showed that disabled people had higher than average levels of unemployment, lower than average incomes as well as significant additional living costs arising from their disability (Office of Population Censuses and Surveys, 1988 and 1989).

The emergence of an organised lobby

The pattern of development in Britain was different from that in the US. In America the civil rights movement that had begun to campaign against racial discrimination in the 1950s extended in the 1960s and 1970s to include women and disabled people. According to a number of commentators (Oliver and Barnes, 1991; De Jong, 1983) this was significant on two grounds. First it associated disability with civil rights, secondly it offered social protest action as a means of achieving those rights.

Two pieces of legislation stand out in America and both are attributable, in large part, to the pressure brought to bear by the civil rights movement. The first was the inclusion of Section 504 in the *Rehabilitation Act 1973*. This makes it illegal for federally-funded schemes or organisations to discriminate against individuals on grounds of disability when employing staff.

The second and more far-reaching piece of legislation was the *Americans with Disabilities Act 1990* which effectively extended the provisions of the earlier legislation to the private sector. Specifically it prohibits discrimination in employment; in public services; in many private services, such as shops, cinemas, restaurants and schools; and in telecommunications. It is widely perceived as a major advance. Senator Edward Kennedy is reported as saying that it is 'a bill of rights for the disabled and America will be a better and fairer nation because of it'. President Bush, who gave the Bill his strong support, declared 'Let the shameful walls of exclusion come tumbling down'.

The American experience has helped to stimulate a significant campaign in Britain for anti-discrimination legislation. During the 1980s the campaign coalesced around an association of Voluntary Organisations for Anti-Discrimination Legislation.

One characteristic of this campaign has been the growing distinction that has emerged between organisations *of* disabled people and organisations *for* them. Organisations *of* disabled people are run by, and are directly accountable to, disabled people. Organisations *for* disabled people are run by non-disabled people and are considered to be unrepresentative.

Some organisations for disabled people continue to be based on the medical model of disability. The British Council of Organisations of Disabled People (BCODP) was formed in 1981 to represent the interests of the organisations *of* disabled people. Ten years later it had over 120 organisations in membership, representing over 250,000 disabled people.

One of the issues that BCODP has campaigned about is the charitable dimension of service provision for disabled people. Many of the service providers trace their origins back to a time when Victorian attitudes defined the nature of charitable activities aimed at disabled people. These attitudes were firmly based in the individual model of disability and are clearly unacceptable to BCODP and other groups that represent disabled people who argue that those institutional attitudes persist. Here it is important to draw a distinction between charities (in the Victorian sense) and the voluntary sector which, with its independence and scope for control by disabled people, is seen to offer a real alternative to service provision by the state.

Pressures for anti-discrimination legislation

By the middle of the 1980s a discernible pressure for anti-discrimination legislation was building up. BCODP had become reasonably well established, as had a growing number of radical groups controlled by disabled people. The Independent Living Movement was demonstrating clearly that disabled people themselves were well able to provide for their own needs, given sufficient cash resources. Yet anti-discrimination legislation was not yet on the mainstream political agenda.

In 1982, Jack Ashley MP began a series of attempts to introduce legislation by means of a Private Member's Bill. The latest in this series was introduced by Dr Roger Berry MP in 1994. In every case the Bills have been opposed on the grounds that the basic premise was essentially negative; that it was very difficult to define disability; that it would be costly and that a better approach was through education, persuasion and targeted legislation, not through the granting of rights (Bynoe, 1991).

The legislation that was introduced by the government, the *Disabled Persons (Services, Consultation and Representation) Act 1986*, failed to address the need for anti-discrimination legislation and the government has since been criticised for its lack of commitment to the provisions in the Act (Oliver, 1991). More recently a consultation paper on employment for disabled people identified both the existence of the problem and the need to legislate against it. This was, however, dismissed by employers' organisations as impractical, ineffective and too expensive (Bynoe, 1991).

The campaign continues. In addition to Private Members' Bills, a number of other devices – such as Adjournment Debates and Early Day Motions – have been used to bring the matter to the attention of both the Lords and the Commons.

The House of Commons Select Committee on Employment recommended in 1991 that 'the government should explore urgently the possibility of equal opportunities legislation for the employment of people with disabilities' (House of Commons, 1991). The matter has been pressed by a wide range of organisations including the Manpower Services Commission, the National Advisory Council on Employment of Disabled People, the Trades Union Congress and, of course, the disability organisations.

In 1994 the Minister for Disabled People published the government's latest recommendations following the defeat of Dr Roger Berry's Bill. This takes things a little further towards the demands of the disability lobby while holding back from full anti-discrimination legislation. It remains to be seen what the outcome of the Parliamentary process will be.

The issue has growing public support and it seems unlikely to go away. Each successive attempt to legislate attracts broader support and more intensive publicity. It seems inevitable that sooner or later some form of equal opportunities legislation for disabled people will be enacted.

When that happens it will reinforce the need for effective information and advice services to enable disabled people to exercise the rights they have won. Experience in the USA suggests that awarding people rights is only the first step (Zarb, 1994). People then have to be made aware of their rights and then helped to exercise them

References

Bynoe, Ian (1991) 'The case for anti-discrimination legislation' *In Equal rights for disabled people: the case for a new law.* Institute for Public Policy Research

Committee on Restrictions against Disabled People (1982) *Report of the Committee.* HMSO

Cook, J and Mitchell, P (1982) *Putting teeth into the Act: a history of attempts to enforce the provisions of section 2 of the Chronically Sick and Disabled Persons Act 1970.* RADAR

De Jong, G (1983) 'Defining and implementing the independent living concept' *In* N Crewe and I Zola (editors) *Independent living for physically disabled people.* Jossey-Bass

House of Commons (1991) *Session 1990-91. Paper Number 35.* HMSO

Office of Population Censuses and Surveys (1988 and 1989) *Reports on disability* (Five reports). HMSO

Oliver, Mike (1991) 'Speaking out: disabled people and state welfare' *In* Gillian Dalley (editor) *Disability and social policy.* Policy Studies Institute

Oliver, Mike and Barnes, Colin (1991) 'Discrimination, disability and welfare: from needs to rights' *In Equal rights for disabled people: the case for a new law.* Institute for Public Policy Research

Zarb, Gerry (1994) *Removing disabling barriers.* Policy Studies Institute

3   Information and citizenship

The notion put forward by the National Consumer Council that information was the fourth right of citizenship (National Consumer Council, 1977) has been endorsed by much of the social legislation enacted during the 1980s and 1990s. Changes in the law governing education, social services and the health services have all introduced a requirement for service providers to make information available so that consumers know what is available and can exercise choice over the services they receive.

In the late 1960s the Consumers' Association pioneered the provision of impartial information about goods and services. Through the publication of test results in *Which?* it became possible for consumers to select the products that best met their needs and their budgets. A degree of objectivity had been introduced into the commercial marketplace.

The principle was readily adopted by a government that emphasised individuality and the need to shift the balance of power away from the providers of public services and towards consumers. They recognised that without information about the services on offer, consumer choice was illusory. Accordingly they included information provisions in a range of pieces of legislation and, through official guidance, exhorted service providers to extend the range of information available to consumers.

A duty to provide or a right to receive

When faced with the need to make more information available to consumers, a government has two choices: it can give consumers a right to receive information on the services available to them; or it can place a duty on the service providers to make information available. On balance, the government has chosen the second option (Moore and Steele, 1991).

There are, however, a small number of notable instances where individuals have been given the right of access to information. The *Data Protection Act 1984* gives individuals the right to see copies of the information that organisations hold about them. The sixth principle on which the legislation is based states that:

> Individuals have the right to be told whether or not a data user holds information about them. If such information is held, individuals have the right of access to the information and the right to have incorrect data corrected or erased.

The Act places a range of duties and obligations on data users but is significant for the rights it accords to individuals.

The *Local Government (Access to Information) Act 1985* and the *Access to Health Records Act 1990* also give individuals the right of access to information. In the first case it is information about the meetings and processes of the local authority and the right to attend the authority's meetings. In the second it is a right of access to the individual's medical records.

Apart from these instances, British citizens have almost no rights to receive or to have access to information. Instead, service providers have been placed under a range of duties to provide information.

This duty to provide has become a common feature of social legislation. The *Chronically Sick and Disabled Persons Act 1970* placed an obligation on local authorities to publish information about their services 'from time to time'. This was extended by the *Disabled Persons (Services, Consultation and Representation) Act 1986* which required local authorities to ensure that all disabled people using its services are informed about other services provided by the authority and by other organisations.

More recently the *Children Act 1989* and the *NHS and Community Care Act 1990* have imposed a duty to publish information about their services and about their community care plans (Steele and others, 1993).

Similar legal obligations have been placed on housing authorities to publish annual reports on their activities; on education authorities to publish information on examination results; and on health authorities to publish information on waiting lists. The process is beginning to extend beyond the public sector and private companies, along with public sector bodies, now have a duty to publish certain environmental information under the *Environmental Protection Act*.

This requirement to publish information in the consumer interest has become closely associated with the charter movement: the attempt to codify the entitlements and legitimate expectations of consumers in their dealings with providers of goods and services. Thus, health authorities are required under the *Patients Charter* to provide a consumer health information service.

These developments have undoubtedly resulted in a much greater volume of information being made available. They do, however, raise a number of issues. The first concerns objectivity and independence. One of the great strengths of *Which?* has been the fact that the information contained in it is compiled, analysed and published independently of the providers of the goods and services. Much of the value inherent in the information arises from this objectivity and independence. And it is likely that, as citizenship information comes to be used more intensively, so there will be calls for a similar degree of independence.

The second issue concerns the degree of analysis and the use to which the information is put. Again *Which?* provides an interesting comparison. Here information about a number of different products is presented in a standard format that permits easy comparison. There is also a commentary associated with the hard data to ease interpretation and to provide some form of summary or recommendation. Contrast this with the very basic information about the residential care homes that is available from most local authority social services departments. There is arguably a need for an agency to analyse the basic data and to publish the results in ways that enable consumers to make easy comparisons.

The need for such comparisons has been recognised in relation to information about education and health service waiting times. Here the responsible government department collects the information and publishes it in the form of league tables. These have attracted considerable criticism on the grounds that the raw data can be misleading. What is needed is a greater degree of analysis and interpretation to enable people to make properly informed decisions.

It also has to be recognised that few of us have the inclination or the capacity to collect, process and use all the information that is available to us as information-intensive citizens. There is a need for specialist agencies to collect and process the information and to make it available on demand as and when required.

Even that, however, will probably be insufficient. The experience of advice services suggests that information alone is seldom sufficient to enable people to solve the problems that they face. What is required is help to interpret the information and to apply it to the circumstances of the individual; advice on the best course of action to take and direct assistance in dealing with the service provider.

It is highly likely, therefore, that the steady increase in the amount of citizenship information available will lead to further demand for advice services.

Underlying this provision of citizenship information is a more fundamental contradiction. Having, as a citizen, a right to information is very far from having a right to receive a service and even further from having a right to choose between different options. The experience of community care since its introduction provides ample evidence of this. Potential service users have a range of rights to information about services. They do not, though, have a right to receive the services to which they may feel they are entitled. It would seem that they do not even have a right to the services that care managers believe they need – they have to make do with the services that can be provided from the budgets that are made available. In this they seldom have any opportunity to choose between alternatives.

The provision of information for citizenship needs, therefore, to be seen realistically. It is an important step forward but one which is limited in its effect. Well-informed citizens may be better able to make choices but those choices only become a reality if the level of provision exceeds the demand for it.

References

Moore, Nick and Steele, Jane (1991) *Information-intensive Britain: an analysis of the policy issues*. Policy Studies Institute

National Consumer Council (1977) *The fourth right of citizenship: a review of local advice services*

Steele, Jane and others (1993) *Informing people about social services*. Policy Studies Institute

4   The path to NDIP

The National Disability Information Project has been shaped by the pattern of advice services; by the movement towards equal opportunities for disabled people and by contemporary beliefs about information and citizenship. It has had to fit into an existing pattern of provision and, like a new employee joining a going concern, has had to adjust to well-established ways of working. To be successful it was necessary, to a great extent, to be defined by others before asserting the project's own identity.

The process of definition, however, began a number of years before NDIP was actually launched. First came an awareness that there was a need to do something about disability information. This prompted an investigation by Coopers and Lybrand, the management consultants. Their recommendations were discussed and further refined into a fundable demonstration project by a different group of consultants – PE International. The project was then formally launched in the summer of 1991.

Many of the parameters that have determined the course of the project were established over this period. It is, therefore, useful to review some of the steps that were taken and to consider the thinking that lay behind them.

Coopers and Lybrand
In early 1988 Coopers and Lybrand were called in by the Department of Health and Social Security and asked to 'examine and report on the basic information needs of disabled people, their carers and service providers.'

The request did not come out of the blue. In 1981 the International Year of Disabled People, which was supported by the Department of Health and Social Security, had focused attention on the information needs of disabled people. One of the organisations to emerge from the International Year's activities was the National Information Forum which had as its main function the promotion and improvement of information services for disabled people.

The Department had also become increasingly aware of the amount of money that was channelled into information-provision activities through the Section 64 grants to national disability organisations. Some of these, like the Disabled Living Foundation, had information provision as one of their major activities. Others, like the RNIB or RADAR, provided information as part of a broader remit.

The Department was concerned to ensure that this money was being used as effectively as possible. It needed to be sure that there was no unnecessary duplication. It also needed to be sure that there were no significant gaps in provision.

Questions were also asked about the relationship between the national providers of information and the local information and advice services. The Department contributed to the headquarters costs of DIAL UK with its network that then extended to over 50 local advice centres. This network was clearly set to expand and there was uncertainty about how it fitted with activities at national level.

Developments were also taking place in another government department. The Department of Trade and Industry had established a Technical Liaison Group as part of its Concerned Technology Programme. This Liaison Group was actively exploring the scope for using information technology to overcome some of the information management and communication problems associated with national information provision for disabled people. A view was emerging that technology could provide a powerful solution to at least some of the problems faced by the national information providers.

There was even a European dimension. The European Commission had recently announced the creation of HANDYNET, an online, European-wide information service for disabled people. The Department was having to consider how the British information system could fit in with this European development.

The conditions were clearly right for an investigation and the contract was awarded to Coopers and Lybrand.

The precise terms of reference for the investigation were:

- To report on what is known about the information needs of disabled people, their carers and those who provide services for them.

- To examine existing systems, computer based and other, for meeting those needs and assess their effectiveness including any gaps or duplication.

- To identify the possible options for improving existing arrangements, to assess their likely cost-effectiveness and possible sources of finance, and to consider the feasibility of establishing a framework of computer-based disability information.

The Coopers and Lybrand team had a big job to do and a short period of time – two months – in which to do it. They undertook a brief literature review and they consulted a range of individuals and organisations, including national information providers, the National Information Forum, and local and health authorities. They have since been criticised for failing to consult sufficiently among the advice service network, although they did talk to officials from DIAL UK and NACAB. They also conducted a limited postal survey of information providers.

Broadly, the report recommended that urgent action by the Department of Health and Social Security was required to improve the provision of information for disabled people at national and local level (Coopers and Lybrand, 1988).

At the national level they recommended work to establish 'a national framework for the provision of information services'. This fell a long way short of 'the framework of computer-based disability information' that was mentioned in the terms of reference. Coopers and Lybrand felt that this represented an over-optimistic view of the contribution that information technology could make and was unrealistic because of the considerable variation in the levels of technological skill and the extent to which technology was used within the national information providers. A very substantial amount of work, linked to significant levels of investment, would have been required to bring them to a position where the kind of information exchange envisaged in the terms of reference became possible.

Instead, they recommended the creation of a framework of common data standards, agreed performance measures, guidelines for the structure of information and support for innovation. This would provide a basis for possible future development of common computer-based services even though these were not feasible at that time.

At the local level they recommended the creation of federations of information providers. It is worth re-stating the key tasks that the report specifies for the federations:

- To set up effective liaison machinery between agencies to ensure coordination and prevent unnecessary duplication.

- To manage and steer the development and implementation of local systems.

- To identify gaps in provision and to develop strategies for bridging them.

- To provide signposts for people with disabilities, carers and service providers to available information systems, including information about the nature and scope of systems and the means of access; such signposts may be individuals acting as information brokers.

- To ensure that systems are monitored and evaluated for effectiveness.

- To ensure that systems are 'consumer-led', that is that the views of people with disabilities and their carers are an integral part of systems development and provision.

- To undertake surveys of the extent and nature of disability in the local area.

- To secure adequate funding from local and national sources, including the pursuit of commercial options.

It is not clear where the concept of the federations comes from. It does not appear to flow naturally from the analysis contained in the report. Nor does the concept seem to have been derived from any particular examples studied by the project team. Indeed, the basis of federations is acknowledged to require further clarification – the report recommends that immediate steps should be taken to 'define the concept in more detail'. This lack of clarity about what is meant by a federation continues to this day.

The Coopers and Lybrand report can be criticised on three main grounds. It failed to perceive that multi-agency working would lead to tension, delay and a lack of progress. It failed to take adequate account of the needs and aspirations of disabled people, particularly in the context of the emerging awareness of equal opportunities for disabled people. And it failed to take account of the role of advice agencies and the nature of the service they provided.

The failure to comprehend the difficulties associated with multi-agency working was unfortunate. The very different organisational cultures of the statutory and voluntary sector make it difficult to establish effective joint working arrangements. Added to this is the complexity of the funding arrangements: the statutory sector is, almost inevitably, going to be the main source of funds. This introduces a significant imbalance into any joint operation.

The failure to make full allowance for disabled people's needs and aspirations can be attributed to the fact that the analysis contained in the report, and the solutions based upon it, are firmly rooted in an individual or medical model of disability. Nowhere in the report is there any mention of the need to consider control by disabled people or the role that disabled people could play in the design and delivery of services. The closest the report comes to such a concept is to acknowledge that services should be '"consumer-led", that is that the views of people with disabilities and their carers are an integral part of systems development and provision'. The report does, however, acknowledge at one point that 'the establishment of self-help groups for many areas of disability has created some good responses.'

The failure to understand the nature and role of advice services is less explicable. The Coopers and Lybrand team spoke to representatives of DIAL UK and the citizens advice bureaux service but clearly did not appreciate the nature of advice work. At one point in the report they refer to 'local advice centres such as post offices, libraries and citizens advice bureaux'. To regard post offices and libraries as advice centres reflects a considerable misunderstanding of what advice services are about.

It is also interesting to note that there is no reference to specialist advice services for disabled people, notably the then growing network of DIALs. Such services clearly play an important role in meeting two of the requirements specified in the report: the ability to take a holistic view of a disabled person's information needs; and the ability to act as an information broker, calling on a range of different primary sources of information. To fail to take them into account represents a major weakness of the report.

These criticisms aside, the report aroused considerable interest, particularly among groups interested in developing local information services for disabled people, even if it met with some resistance among the established providers of local advice services. A number of services based on the federation concept have had their origins credited to the report – the Disablement Information Service in Surrey, the Birmingham Information Federation and the Oxford Disability Information Project, to name but three.

More particularly, the report provided the basis for the detailed planning of the project that was to become NDIP.

Shaping the project

After a gap of nearly two years, the Department of Health decided to proceed with the kind of development project that was envisaged by the Coopers and Lybrand report. To assist them with their planning, they commissioned another management consultancy, PE International, to define the parameters of a project to test some of the Coopers and Lybrand recommendations, particularly those concerned with local federations, and generally to assist the improvement of information services.

One of the issues explored in some depth by PE International was the scope for designating some of the national information providers as

Common Service Providers whose databases could be linked and accessed directly by local federations. This work demonstrated the wide variations in the use of technology among the national information providers and the high costs associated with any attempt to bring about the degree of compatibility and standardisation that would be required. As a consequence, this aspect of the development work was scaled down considerably in the detailed planning of NDIP and was subsequently dropped on the advice of the project steering group.

PE International undertook to clarify the concept of information federations. They identified three possible models: centralised, radial and cascade.

- The *centralised* model was based on a single enquiry point which would hold and maintain a database and use it to respond to questions. The federation members would act as a steering group ensuring that the information provided was appropriate to local needs.

- The *radial* model would have a central enquiry point linked to satellite enquiry points, each satellite being a member of the federation. The federation members collectively would act as the steering group for the federation.

- The *cascade* model would have satellites that were not single organisations but sub- or mini-federations. This model was thought to be appropriate for large counties.

We will return to these models when analysing the experience of the pilot projects that were selected to become part of NDIP.

The basic framework was set. The National Disability Project would have twin aims: to improve services at local and national level. The project would be managed by an independent group who would work with a number of local federations. The project team would also be required to work with national information providers and to coordinate their efforts.

The launch

The National Disability Information Project was launched in the summer of 1991. Officials from the Department consulted a number of groups, including national information providers, the main advice agencies and organisations representing disabled people. On the basis of this consultation they drew up firm plans for the project.

The budget was £1 million a year for three financial years – 1991-92 to 1993-94. This budgetary timescale presented the first problem. The clock had begun to tick away. The project was launched as quickly as possible but even so it was not possible to start spending the first year's money until well into the financial year.

The budgetary timescale also meant that, while NDIP was envisaged as a three-year project, the pilot projects were not selected until September 1991 and it was, therefore, only possible to issue contracts to the participants for the remaining two and a half financial years. In the event, an additional sum of money was made available to allow the project to carry on for the first half of a fourth financial year – until the end of September 1994. This effectively restored the money 'lost' at the end of 1991-92 and meant that the project ran for a full three years.

In late June 1991 the Department invited, through a series of public advertisements, local federations of disability information providers to apply to become pilot projects within the National Disability Information Project. The deadline for applications was tight – groups had little more than a month in which to respond – but this was inevitable, given the budgetary timescale.

A number of requirements were placed on the potential applicants. The federation had to include participants from both the statutory and voluntary sectors. One of the voluntary sector agencies had to agree to take on responsibility for managing the money as the Department faced various administrative complexities when making payments to local and health authorities. Other than these two requirements, potential federations had considerable scope to interpret the meaning of a disability information federation. Indeed, the Department encouraged a wide range of approaches from both established and newly formed federations in order to be able to test the concept in a variety of different ways.

The response to the advertisement was considerable. More than 100 groups applied. Some of these, however, were from Wales and Scotland and were excluded as the project was restricted to England. That left 98 applications that were considered. Of these, 12 were selected to become pilot projects. This was more than had been envisaged originally. The higher number was made possible simply because individual federation budgets were rather lower than had been expected.

Applicants were notified of the outcome in September and those that were successful were encouraged to open for business as quickly as possible.

From the outset, various attempts were made to emphasise that the 12 had been selected to demonstrate a range of different approaches in different parts of the country. They had not been chosen because they were the best. 'This is not a beauty contest' became a phrase that was often repeated.

The timescale for appointing the project team was very similar. A specification was sent out to six organisations inviting them to tender for the work. The deadline was the same as for the pilot federations – noon on 31 July. Applicants were interviewed in August and the contract was awarded to the Policy Studies Institute in September.

The Department appointed a steering committee to oversee the development of the project. It was felt to be important to avoid potential conflicts of interest. Accordingly the committee comprised individuals who had an interest in disability information but who were not closely associated with any of the organisations, national or local, that might benefit from NDIP.

The work by PE International had emphasised the need for the project to be thoroughly evaluated. It was felt that the evaluation should be independent of the project itself and, accordingly, in mid-1992 the Research Branch of the Department commissioned the Research Institute for Consumer Affairs to undertake the task of evaluating the processes and the outcomes of the project.

The public launch of NDIP took place in November 1991 in the International Convention Centre in Birmingham. The Department organised a conference on information for disabled people which was attended by over three hundred people. The Minister for Disabled People, Nicholas Scott, opened the conference, launching NDIP in the process.

The Birmingham conference provided the first opportunity for people to see what the pilot projects were planning to achieve. The conference also provided an opportunity for the various interest groups to begin the process of trying to shape the project to meet their particular requirements. Some had been doing this throughout the formative stages. From now on the process became a little more public.

The one remaining task was to establish the working aims and objectives for NDIP. The overall aims were established from the outset by the Department. They were:

- *Nationally,* to improve the effectiveness of the national information providers and to promote greater coordination.

- *Locally,* to encourage the development of effective local information and advice services.

The conference provided an opportunity to develop more specific objectives. The first draft of these was considered by the project steering group and by the pilot federations. A slightly revised version was published for general consultation in the project's newsletter, after which they were adopted as the basic framework for the project. They were:

- To ensure that all services fully meet the needs of their users.

- To ensure that there is an adequate supply of appropriate information.

- To ensure that there is an even pattern of provision throughout the country.

- To ensure that there is an adequate and stable source of funding for the information services.

- To ensure that services are provided by well-trained, and where appropriate, well-paid staff.

- To ensure that information service providers have access to cheap, reliable and effective information systems.

- To ensure that the development of information services for disabled people does not take place in isolation.

- To ensure that there is an infrastructure which will encourage and support further development.

Clearly, these represent far-reaching aspirations that could not be fully achieved during the life of NDIP. They did, however, indicate the direction that NDIP was to take.

References
Coopers and Lybrand (1988) *Information needs of disabled people, their carers and service providers.* Department of Health and Social Security

Part II

The players in the National Disability Information Project

From the outset it was stressed that the National Disability Information Project was more than the twelve pilot projects. It would have been easy to think of NDIP as a rather closed development, at the end of which it would be possible to produce useful guidance and an interesting report. Instead the project set out to be much wider – a development that would try to encompass all individuals and organisations seeking to improve information for disabled people. When describing the component parts of NDIP it is, therefore, necessary to include those whose involvement was indirect.

The organisations that were directly involved are easy to identify. They are the twelve pilot projects, the project team and the evaluation group. Two other categories of organisations were less directly involved. They were the national information providers and the local disability information and advice services, some of which had applied unsuccessfully to become pilot projects. When considering these local services it is also necessary to take into account the various networks that support them and represent their interests.

To understand NDIP and to begin to assess the impact that it has made, it is necessary to consider the nature of each of these different groups and to appreciate the context within which they were operating.

Part II – Contents

5   The pilot projects

As we have seen, the selection of the pilot projects was not a beauty contest. Far from being an attempt to choose the best services then in operation, the selection was based on a number of criteria intended to provide a balanced range of different approaches that could be tested and compared.

The Department tried to achieve a reasonably even distribution across the country – between urban and rural areas. They selected some projects that were well established and others that were completely new – projects that had only come into being with the call for applications. Some projects emphasised their intended use of information technology, others placed more emphasis on people-based services. The Department also tried to ensure that the three models identified by PE International – centralised, radial and cascade – were represented.

The result was a group of twelve projects that are nothing if not different from one another. This high degree of variation is one of the strengths of the project. It shows that a range of different approaches is possible. It is also one of the weaknesses as it is extremely difficult to compare any of the projects with the any other. It is therefore hard to come to firm conclusions about which approaches work and which do not – what may be very successful in one set of circumstances may prove to be unworkable elsewhere.

It is worth considering the main characteristics, activities and achievements of each project in turn.

The Berkshire Disability Information Network
The Berkshire Disability Information Network (BDIN) is based on a small central unit with six satellite federations. Each of these local federations is responsible for collecting information and passing it on to the central unit for inclusion in the database, for identifying sites for information services for disabled people and, more generally, for promoting awareness of information for disabled people.

BDIN was established in 1990 as part of the Oxford Disability Information Project. In its early stages it was led strongly by the local authority, with significant inputs from both the county library and the social services departments. The two local health authorities are also involved as are a range of voluntary sector organisations.

Aims

The aim of the Berkshire Disability Information Network is:

- To improve the quality and accessibility of information for people with disabilities, their carers and service professionals throughout Berkshire.

Within this broad aim the project has seven specific objectives:

- To set up 18 fully accessible disability information centres across Berkshire in existing information outlets.

- To establish six local federations of information providers to coordinate information, identify sites for information centres and to support them.

- To set up a central database of information that could be accessed by the information centres.

- To set up quality standards for both disability information and how it is communicated.

- To set up a consumer group to monitor and evaluate the service.

- To identify sources of funding to ensure the long term prospects for the network.

- To ensure that every household in Berkshire is made aware of what and where information is to be found.

BDIN as such does not provide a direct public information service, nor does it offer advice. The intention is to work with existing providers and to strengthen their information resources.

Main characteristics

BDIN began with an ambitious programme of work which proved to be unattainable. In part this was the product of an over-optimistic assessment of what could be achieved in the time available. Mainly, however, it was attributable to the organisational structure that was originally adopted. The steering committee tried to do most of the work. Some staff were recruited on relatively short contracts for specific tasks but this produced fragmentation and a lack of continuity. It also placed a heavy burden on steering committee members, most of whom had a full range of commitments elsewhere.

The result was that early plans to establish local federations; to identify suitable locations for information centres; to design and build a database; to set out accreditation standards for the information centres; to develop training programmes; to undertake research into user needs and into the role of GPs as information providers and to gather a wide range of information all took much longer than expected.

After making various attempts to overcome the lack of progress, a decision was taken to appoint a project manager and to delegate to him or her the responsibility for taking executive action. The result has been much steadier and rather faster progress. The project manager and the information officer, working together within a policy framework developed by the executive committee have been able to increase the number of local information services and to improve the quality of the database. BDIN has, however, had to scale down its original goals. Fewer information centres than the 18 that were originally planned have been established – 6 were operational by July 1993, a further four were operational by December 1994 with another three under negotiation. The database plans have also had to be substantially revised.

The future

BDIN is set to continue. The Network has obtained funding through the joint finance arrangements between the health and the local authority. The central database is being extended and improved. The work in the ten information centres will continue while negotiations take place to establish further information centres. The basic structure of a central unit with a number of information centres supported by local federations will continue.

Assessment

The question that must be asked is how much value does BDIN add to the services provided by the information centres? Almost all of the information centres previously provided information and advice to disabled people. Most did so within a generalist framework – the CABx and the community health council – while one did so within the framework provided by a disability organisation. So the ultimate measure of the project must be the degree to which the information and advice services are better now than they were three years ago. Given the limitations on the amount of training that it has been possible to provide, and the problems associated with the database, it is hard to say that the added value is really significant.

Looked at another way, would greater improvements have resulted if the money had been spent directly on the organisations that house the information centres? Each could have stimulated the creation of local federations to support their work but could have used the resources more directly to enhance their service provision.

This points to the conclusion that any central support service is effectively an overhead and it is vital to ensure that the services provided by this overhead are of significant value to those that receive them. The value added by the central services must be greater than the value that could be added by distributing the resources throughout the system. The Berkshire Disability Information Network has yet to demonstrate clearly that this is the case.

Birmingham Information Federation

The Birmingham Information Federation (BIF) brings together a large number of organisations in the city. As federation members they elect a management committee which controls the work of the central team. This team undertakes a range of activities on behalf of the members but does not provide an enquiry service.

The federation was established in 1988 on the initiative of the local authority and as a direct response to the recommendations in the Coopers and Lybrand report. The federation received considerable support in kind from Birmingham City Council Social Services Department. NDIP funding was obtained so that the federation could be developed further.

Aims

BIF aims to improve access to information for disabled people and their carers. More specifically, the project has five objectives:

- To create an extensive network throughout the city of Birmingham of relevant organisations and individuals so that information can be shared more effectively.

- To actively include black and minority ethnic organisations in that network.

- To experiment with using technology to network organisations.

- To be consumer led.

- To research the information needs of people with disabilities and carers within the city.

37

Main characteristics

BIF has always been significant among the 12 pilot projects as the one which is most clearly concerned with networking and communication between members. In doing this BIF has acted as a catalyst and facilitator, and tried to create a culture of accessibility, in which information and ideas are shared, and the quality of information is improved.

The federation has provided a number of its members with computer equipment and has organised training in how to use technology. It has completed a multi-stage research programme into the information needs of disabled people. BIF has produced a promotional video, and is preparing a promotional pack for people with learning disabilities. The federation has also developed a range of services for members including a newsletter and regular meetings.

BIF obtained sponsorship to pilot a signposting information service. The service, called Disability Link Line, was launched in 1993. It directs enquirers to the most appropriate source of assistance.

Following the appointment of a new director, BIF sought to establish methods of working which ensure a greater degree of participation by, and accountability to, disabled people. The federation has also tried to develop a broader range of services. These include disability equality training and community development work.

The future

BIF has obtained funding for three years from joint finance, albeit at a lower level than previously. The funds are not sufficient to cover the full costs of maintaining an office. Instead, a contract has been issued to Disability West Midlands for the provision of services to the federation members.

Assessment

At the outset BIF was intended to be a resource provider to and a supporter of its members. Its early attempts to develop such support were not wholly successful. The supply of computer equipment was, perhaps not surprisingly, well received. Other activities were less successful. Questions have been raised about the value and quality of the research. Certainly the exercise has not generated as much new understanding as was originally hoped. The impact of other activities, such as the promotional video, has probably not been sufficient to justify fully the costs involved.

The Disability Link Line is a potentially valuable service, but the nature of the take-up suggests that a steady volume of publicity is needed to stimulate use of the service. It might be more valuable to devote the energy and resources involved into direct promotion of the services to which referral is made.

It has only been possible to attract long-term funding at a reduced level for the federation. This probably reflects the fact that it is difficult to make a sound case for support services when funders are facing significant pressure to direct resources to those agencies that are directly involved with service provision.

It is difficult to avoid the conclusion that BIF was a federation in search of a role. In part this may have been a result of the attempt to involve as many groups as possible as federation members. With such a diverse group, it was difficult to see what services could be provided to them all. Had membership been more closely restricted, perhaps to the agencies in the city that were directly involved with the provision of information and advice services for disabled people or, alternatively, to the active disability groups, then it might have been easier to define a role for the central unit.

Devon Disability Information and Advice Federation

The Devon Disability Information and Advice Federation (DDIAF) consists of a number of satellite services that provide information direct to the public. Each of these satellite services is a member of the federation. A number of other voluntary and statutory organisations are members of the federation. There is a small central unit that provides support and development services to these satellites but it does not provide a public enquiry service.

The federation was based on a forum that was established in 1988 with the active support of the Plymouth Guild of Community Service. The federation has also benefited from wholehearted support from the county council. DDIAF employs a Coordinator who works closely with staff from other organisations in the federation.

Aims

The aim of DDIAF is, quite simply:

• To provide high quality information and advice services to people with disabilities across the county of Devon.

Main achievements

DDIAF set out to carry out three pieces of work: to produce a monitoring and evaluation package for disability information services; to develop a training package for advice workers and to develop its use of information technology in conjunction with the local authority. In each of these it has been successful.

The monitoring and evaluation package has been developed in close consultation with the federation members and has been extensively tested by them. It has now been made more widely available (Devon Disability Information and Advice Federation, 1994c). The Project Team drew on the Devon experience when compiling its guidelines on evaluation (Simpkins, 1993)

The training package includes a video which has been developed in conjunction with St Loyes School of Occupational Therapy, a federation member. The training package is also generally available (Devon Disability Information and Advice Federation, 1994a).

Before NDIP the federation had a database that was maintained independently by four disability information service centres that were responsible for collating and upgrading information across the county. The database was mounted on a personal computer. NDIP enabled the federation to re-write the database program and to down-load the information onto the county council's mainframe computer. Network links were provided to the four disability information centres. The information was also made available through the county council network to local offices of the social services department. This work was carried out in close collaboration with the local authority. The federation continues to explore the potential for other services to become part of the network. As part of this work, DDIAF have developed a keyword classification scheme (Devon Disability Information and Advice Federation, 1994b). The Disabled Living Foundation's database, DLF Data, is also available to members through the network.

The future

Devon County Council has agreed to continue to fund DDIAF until the end of 1994-95. The broad aims of the federation will remain the same although the emphasis will be placed on consolidating the advances that have been made in the last three years. This will be achieved by ensuring that the developments are fully integrated into the work of the local centres and used as the basis for future progress with other federation members.

Assessment

DDIAF provides concrete evidence of what can be achieved by pooling resources and by building on collective strengths. The scale of resources is relatively modest – only one project worker is employed by the federation, although support in kind, particularly from the county council and the Plymouth Guild, has been considerable.

The project set out with clear aims and objectives and a defined programme of work. This has now been completed and there are tangible results. In this case the value added by the central unit does appear to be greater than the value that would have been added had the resources been divided up between the federation members. What is more, the project coordinator has been able to draw on the particular strengths of federation members and to develop a degree of collaborative working that would have been very difficult to achieve by disparate organisations working cooperatively.

Gateshead Disability Information Project

The Gateshead Disability Information Project (GDIP) does not really have federation members as such. The Project was established jointly by Gateshead MBC Libraries and Arts Service and Gateshead Council on Disability. It is managed primarily by these two organisations with additional input from representatives of two local disability groups. It works with a group of advice agencies in the borough but these do not really constitute a disability information federation. In other respects, GDIP does collect and process information centrally, providing a number of services to advice and disability groups in Gateshead.

A significant element of GDIP is the experimental development and application of interactive compact disc technology to make information more accessible for people with hearing impairments.

Aims

The project aims to improve the provision and accessibility of information for disabled people and their carers in Gateshead. Within this broad aim it has the following specific objectives:

- To establish a disability information service based at the premises of Gateshead Council on Disability and at the Fountain View Resource Centre.

- To work with the Gateshead Forum for Local Advice Groups and others on the production and presentation of relevant information including a database and directory of Support and Self-help groups.

- To establish ways that users and carers can comment on and evaluate local information services.

- To promote the publication of information in a number of different formats.

- To explore the scope for using interactive compact disc technology to make information more accessible for people with hearing impairments.

Main characteristics
The Gateshead project has two main elements: a set of development activities involving work with local groups to develop services and to ensure that these services are evaluated by users; and set of experimental activities exploring the use of CD-i technology as a publishing medium for disabled people.

GDIP has acted as a catalyst in the development of disability information networks in Gateshead. The project has produced a database and directory of over 470 support and self help groups in Gateshead and Newcastle (Gateshead Disability Information Project, 1993a and 1994d). A similar directory has been produced for black and ethnic minority groups (Gateshead Disability Information Project, 1994a).

The project has also produced a newsletter and has undertaken a range of other support tasks with GDIP both facilitating the networking of other local groups and acting as an information resource for a range of disability groups and those working on research about disability.

The aim of the work with CD-i, or interactive compact disc, is to look at the ways that technology can make information on topics of general public interest available to disabled people.

The project has produced two discs. The first was based on RADAR's guide to employment for disabled people (Gateshead Disability Information Project, 1993b), the second is a guide to Gateshead Hospital (Gateshead Disability Information Project, 1994c). Information is given in British Sign Language, spoken English and sub-titles. A major innovation on the second disk is the ability to choose one of 8 languages, including English and British Sign Language – another is the use of talking icons, which will make the information accessible to people with visual impairments. The discs have been evaluated both in terms of their production and use (Gateshead Disability Information Project, 1993c).

The future
GDIP as such was wound up at the end of NDIP. The work initiated under NDIP, however, continues. Funding has been obtained from the European Commission to continue its work with CD-i. This comes from the TIDE (Technology for Socio-Economic Integration of the Disabled and Elderly)

programme and has involved collaboration with a number of organisations in member states. The funds are for two years and will enable the Libraries and Arts Service to produce three more discs.

The Libraries and Arts Service will also continue the development of disability information services on the local cable television network.

The Council on Disability will continue the compilation of the directories and the newsletter.

In the final year of NDIP funding, both the Council on Disability and the Libraries and Arts Service were asked by the South Tyne Health Commission and Gateshead MBC to tender for the provision of a community care information service. They decided to collaborate again and to submit a joint tender. The bid was successful, although it was on a smaller scale than originally envisaged. It has led to the creation of a new project: the Community Care Information Project and will enable much of GDIP's information work to continue.

Assessment

The Gateshead project has been a success. Both strands of the work have produced tangible results that are of value. The development work supporting information and advice services in Gateshead has proved to be useful. The published directories and the information collections are well used. A measure of the success of this aspect of the work is the fact that long-term funding has been made available jointly by a health commission and the local authority to enable the activity to be continued.

The CD-i work has also been successful. Many lessons have been learned and passed on to others. A measure of the achievement was the successful bid to the European Commission's TIDE programme that will allow the project to continue to develop CD-i.

In short, even though GDIP as originally constituted no longer exists, the work they began has attracted the support of funders and there is every confidence that it will continue to do so.

Gloucestershire GUIDE

GUIDE, the Gloucester Updated Information Service for Disabled or Elderly People conforms to the centralised model of a federation. It is a single, central enquiry point, based in Gloucester Royal Hospital and using a database to provide an enquiry service. The database is used by other information providers in the county. Federation members serve on the steering group for the project although formally management is through Gloucestershire Health – the county health purchasers.

GUIDE was launched about a year before the start of NDIP. It began as an information service for the public and for professionals in the statutory and voluntary sectors concerned with elderly and physically disabled people. Funding was provided for seven years out of the joint finance arrangements. This money was used to employ three staff members, whose primary role it was to develop a database for health and care professionals in the county and to provide an enquiry service.

Additional funding from NDIP enabled GUIDE to extend its service to people with learning difficulties and mental health problems and to support the development of satellite services.

Aims

GUIDE's aims are to improve and maximise the quality and accessibility of information services for elderly people and those with physical disabilities, learning difficulties and mental health problems, their carers and service providers, in a user led, responsive manner.

Main characteristics

More than any of the other pilot projects, GUIDE has the characteristics of the statutory sector. This is perhaps not surprising as more than half their total costs are borne jointly by the local and health authority which delegate to GUIDE their responsibilities for certain aspects of information provision.

The project's main activities are developing and making available the GUIDE information system; providing a direct information service; and liaising with local groups.

GUIDE has put a considerable amount of care and attention into creating two major products: a database of information relating to disability (GUIDE, 1994) and a thesaurus of disability terms (GUIDE, 1993). The thesaurus has been designed to provide an alternative means of accessing information in the information system. Although these products were planned to support GUIDE and its associated organisations within Gloucestershire, recently the project has stepped into a wider arena by offering both products for sale on the open market.

The database is currently available at over 100 access points within Gloucestershire mainly in the statutory sector, but with some PC-based systems in voluntary organisations. It has been developed using the CAIRS text retrieval software. By the end of NDIP the database contained over 4,500 entries. These are updated on an annual cycle. GUIDE planned originally to increase that to over 20,000 but subsequent realisation of the amount of work involved has led them to scale down their expectations.

The database can be accessed in more than one way: through a hierarchical menu-based system using levels through which the enquirer progresses, and through a keyword system which allows the enquirer to go straight to the appropriate entry by relating the term used by the enquirer to the term which accesses the entry. The basis for this keyword system is the thesaurus of terms that GUIDE have developed and published (GUIDE, 1993).

GUIDE planned to expand its network to include groups outside the health service. However, while some liaison work does take place, and staff have been active in, for example, setting up a local one-day conference and exhibition on disability issues and equipment, in general, GUIDE has taken a limited view of what working with local groups means. Principally this has been restricted to providing groups with the database, and with training on how to use it. They have, however, provided support to a range of initiatives in the county, such as a mobile information service on aids and equipment. But they have not established satellites like those in Berkshire or Devon.

GUIDE also limits its public service to the provision of information. It does not set out to provide advice. On complex issues, like a request for assistance with a welfare benefits problem, they refer enquirers to agencies like the local CAB.

The future
The future for GUIDE seems assured. The health authority agreed to make good the shortfall in funding that arose when the NDIP support ended and there are clear expectations of continuing support from joint finance. The project is well established within its agreed objectives and seems set to continue for many years.

Assessment
The nature of the service provided by GUIDE reflects its firm base within the statutory sector. It is a well-resourced project that has produced a relatively sophisticated database of local information that can be accessed by the public, by professionals and by some voluntary agencies. It offers a limited public information service but draws the line at the provision of advice. In certain respects this is understandable given the hospital context within which it operates – medical matters are one area where it is, perhaps, sensible to draw a distinction between information and advice.

It is, however, a service whose ethos has been relatively little influenced by two of the three social forces that we identified in Part I: the development of advice services or the movement towards equal opportunities for disabled people.

Furthermore, the service not been able to make as much progress as initially hoped in extending access to people with learning disabilities and people with mental illness.

Kent Information Federation

The Kent federation was set up from scratch, with the bid to NDIP being put in by a consortium of organisations from the statutory and voluntary sectors. There was a recognition that information provision in Kent was uncoordinated, and that something needed to be done about it.

What was proposed was something similar to the cascade model of a federation identified by PE International, that is to say, a central unit providing a range of services to satellites that were themselves local federations. The central unit of KIF does not, however, provide a public enquiry service: that function is undertaken by the North West Kent DIAL which is based in the same building and is one of the KIF branches.

Aims

The original aims of the Kent Information Federation (KIF) were wide-ranging – to set up a county-wide information service, involving a federation of information providers; to involve carers and users and to ensure that information was provided in ways which would encourage this; to assist Social Services in meeting its requirement to provide information; and to work with GPs and other gatekeepers.

The breadth of these aims has caused problems, mainly because it has been difficult to allocate resources to the competing demands and it has been necessary to spend some time deciding on priorities.

Main characteristics

KIF has a central core of activities that provide development and support services to six local federations. As in Berkshire, it was necessary to develop these federations and, in most cases, to establish information and advice services.

Reaching agreement on the formal structure for KIF was a long process. After considerable discussion, it was decided to establish KIF formally as a county-wide organisation which would contain the local federations (to be known as branches). An alternative structure would have been six independent local federations and a central service, with their mutual dependence managed through contractual arrangements. It follows that, in establishing KIF as a county-wide organisation, it has been necessary to demonstrate to the branches that the service they receive from the centre is worthwhile and to build in safeguards to prevent any loss of control by the branches of their own local finances.

A key element in the service provided to the branches is the database of local information. This is compiled by KIF but, rather than investing time and effort in the development of their own information system, a decision was taken to enter into a contract with the Disability Information Service in Surrey (DISS) which already had a working system. This means that information is collected in Kent, processed and made available by DISS.

In addition to the database, the central office has undertaken work on quality control and has provided a range of training for the branches. The social services department in Dartford and Gravesham provided some resources to develop information services for minority ethnic communities in the area. Consultation with community representatives indicated that they wanted a targeted service to be provided. It seemed possible to offer this through two new day centres for ethnic minority elders and negotiations were opened with the social services department but, so far, it has not been possible to make any progress.

Much time and effort has, however, been taken up with the establishment of the local branches and with the development of the database. The database does, however, provide them with a resource that can be used to generate future income through service contracts with statutory services.

The future

KIF is another federation that seems set to continue. There is a continue problem with money – the federation faces the need to secure funding for both its central activities and to work with the local services to ensure that they are properly financed. Providing that the money can be found, the federation seems set to continue along its development path.

Assessment

KIF clearly demonstrates the cost of multi-agency working. Even with a great amount of goodwill it was necessary to expend very considerable amounts of time and effort in dealing with constitutional, structural and management issues. The matter was further complicated when organisations from both the statutory and voluntary sectors tried to work together. Organisational cultures differ greatly and it was not easy to find quick solutions, particularly when attempting to create an organisation that was controlled by disabled people out of one that, initially at least, was significantly influenced by representatives from a statutory sector that was itself experiencing structural change.

That KIF has managed to create the federation that now exists owes a great deal to the skill, tact and persistence of some of the key individuals who were involved in the process.

Even with skill and good luck, the process of developing local federations and local advice services was a slow one and KIF demonstrated the need to allow adequate time for full consultation and negotiation.

KIF also raised interesting questions about the role of relatively large and sophisticated databases in the provision of information and advice services for disabled people. The creation of such databases is not a task to be undertaken lightly. KIF chose a route that was felt to be the most cost-effective, but even so a great deal of time was spent on system development and on information collection. The result was a product that may hold the key to future funding based on service contracts with the statutory sector. But the opportunity cost must be considered. If the resources had instead been diverted to other forms of support for the local federations – to the provision of training in advice work, perhaps – it seems possible that the net return to the local federations, and to the disabled people who will turn to them for information and advice, would have been greater.

Manchester Disability Information Service

The Manchester Disability Information Service (MDIS) operates within a city which has a very active disabled people's movement and, from the outset, MDIS has been committed to control by disabled people. MDIS has also always intended to develop the use of information technology to improve access to information.

MDIS has never set out either to assemble an information collection, or to provide an enquiry service. Instead it has sought to strengthen information and advice provision for disabled people in a range of less direct ways.

Aims

MDIS experienced a number of difficulties in recruiting staff at the beginning of the project and, indeed, was the last of the pilots to become operational. Because of this it was necessary to revise the project aims and objectives in the Autumn of 1992. At this stage it was agreed to abandon any attempt to provide a public information service. The management committee agreed the following aims:

- To coordinate and collate information from a wide variety of sources.

- To ensure the dissemination of information in appropriate accessible formats.

- To develop new information sources and innovative ways of disseminating information.

- To establish a network of links between information providers to coordinate the provision of information relevant to disability.

- To enable the participation of a wide spectrum of disabled people in the development of information provision.

Within the framework established by these aims, they set out a number of specific objectives:

- To carry out a consultation process with disabled people, disabled people's groups, carers and service providers about their information needs.

- To carry out a survey of information providers concerning information that they hold relevant to disabled people and current usage of the service by disabled people.

- To set up and maintain a database system to develop a central resource of information currently not available and to disseminate it to the appropriate information providers.

- To support and assist information providers in making their information accessible to all disabled people.

- To give disabled people an opportunity to develop skills in the use of information technology to both access and exchange information.

- To act as consultants or advisers to information providers in making information accessible to all disabled people.

Main characteristics

Two of the main features of MDIS are its control by disabled people and its use of technology to improve access to information. All of the staff were disabled people, and the majority of the management committee members represent disabled people's groups. The philosophy of MDIS is very much geared towards improving access and establishing the rights of disabled people in society.

The use of technology involved using the publicly accessible Manchester Host information network as communications medium for disabled people. MDIS mounted a range of information on a bulletin board on the Host – the NDIP newsletters, for example, were posted there. MDIS encouraged disabled people to make use of the networks to obtain information. The amount of information made available in this way was, however, limited and no attempt was made to evaluate the extent to which it was used. This work was hampered by factors outside the control of MDIS. At one stage, there was a proposal to establish a service, called Disnet, specifically aimed at disabled people. MDIS supported this proposal and intended to make it one of the vehicles for their information provision activities. But Disnet has yet to become fully operational.

The main focus of MDIS activities became to support other providers in Manchester. Staff identified a need for this type of activity because of poor coordination and, in some case, rivalry, between some of the existing groups. It was hoped that MDIS networking activities, its newsletter and signposting service would help to develop a better coordinated network. In practice MDIS failed to become adequately integrated into either of the two communities that it might have worked with. These were the advice services in the city and the network of disability groups, most of which were part of the two networks (Manchester Disability Forum and the Greater Manchester Coalition of Disabled People) that were instrumental in putting forward the original NDIP application.

Two surveys were launched by the project. One was to assess information needs. This was administered through disability groups and through the local authority social services and education departments. The other survey attempted to identify where the gaps were in the information held by organisations. Neither survey produced any conclusive results.

One positive piece of work was an investigation of the ways in which information technology can be used to overcome information access problems experienced by disabled people (Marsh, 1994).

The future
MDIS has been unable to obtain the funds needed for the service to continue as originally envisaged. The search for financial support continues and a basic level of service is provided by the project worker supported by volunteers. Funding for the project worker has been provided by a range of small donations from different sources. The search for a realistic level of financial support continues. The long-term prospects, however, are not promising.

Assessment

The experience in Manchester has not been encouraging. Relatively little was achieved and it is hard to point to any ways in which information and advice services for disabled people have been significantly improved as a result of its work.

Four factors appear to have limited the success of MDIS. The first concerns the aims and objectives of the project. The initial aims were ambitious and it was accepted at an early stage that it would be necessary to scale things down to something that was more manageable. It was not easy to do this, yet the need became more pressing as the recruitment and staffing problems became more severe.

During the life of MDIS there were significant changes in the composition of the management committee. All were for good reasons but there was an inevitable lack of continuity. This meant that, for significant periods, the project lacked a sense of direction and, on occasions, the staff lacked motivation. Both are crucial in a time-limited project that has set itself ambitious targets.

The situation was compounded by the difficulties that MDIS experienced in recruiting staff. The project seldom had a full complement of staff and the high turnover again meant that there was a lack of continuity. It proved difficult to recruit staff who had experience in information and advice work.

Finally, the project failed to engage with the advice sector in the city. Manchester is fortunate in that it has a very active network of advice agencies. Had MDIS been able to establish a working contact with this network it might have been possible to improve in the accessibility, in all senses, of that network for disabled people.

The combination of these factors meant that MDIS was unable to achieve its goals.

Norfolk Disability Information Federation

The Norfolk Disability Information Federation (NDIF) intends ultimately to develop a federal structure. The project is, however, managed by representatives from the organisations that came together to make the application for NDIP funds. Further, a decision was taken that the central team should provide support services to local groups and to the branches, but that they should not provide a direct information service to the public.

Aims

NDIF's aims are:

- To ensure that all disabled people and their carers throughout the county of Norfolk receive the information they require to enable them to live as independently as possible.

- To incorporate the knowledge base, skills and resources of all participating individuals, groups and organisations into a dynamic but composite information bank, for their mutual benefit.

- To give particular attention to the need to make information fully accessible to people with a sensory disability.

Main characteristics

Given the geography of Norfolk it was felt that the most appropriate role for NDIF would be to act as a catalyst, identifying needs and seeking ways in which they can be met.

NDIF began by mapping levels of information need and existing levels of service provision throughout the county. Reports were prepared on each district, identifying the service providers, both among advice agencies and among disability groups, and their needs (Norfolk Disability Information Federation, 1994c). From this it quickly became apparent that disability groups needed training in information and advice skills, while the advice workers needed disability equality training.

A decision was taken, after some debate, to accept a contract from the local authority to compile a database of local disability information that could be mounted on the authority's computer information service, to be made available in libraries and social services offices. The compilation of this database has represented a major task.

NDIF established a sensory disability group to identify and discuss the needs of people with sensory impairments. The group has conducted a survey of local organisations, organised two training sessions and has compiled a guide to services in Norfolk for people with sensory impairments as well as guidelines in presenting information for people with sensory impairments (Norfolk Disability Information Federation, 1994a and 1994b).

The Federation also produces a newsletter which is very well received. It disseminates information to local groups, both advice services and disability groups, and encourages the development of services.

The future
The prospects for NDIF are good. Following the end of NDIP support, funds have been made available from joint finance to enable the federation to continue. A business plan is being prepared as part of a strategy to obtain long-term support from the Norfolk County Council Social Services Department. Other sources of funding are being explored to finance specific activities or publications.

Assessment
Unlike Manchester, NDIF has benefited from stability and continuity of project staff and a clear set of aims and objectives. These factors have, no doubt, helped it to achieve all that it has.

The work of mapping provision, and the contacts and activities that have resulted from this work, have been significant. It does, however, require considerable effort to develop the range of services that would be required to capitalise on the opportunities that have been revealed. The work with the sensory impairment groups shows what can be achieved.

Once again, however, resources have been diverted towards the compilation of a database. The value of such a database to the groups that are in a position to deliver information and advice services to disabled people has to be questioned, particularly in the light of the activities that have to be forgone in order to accommodate the work.

North East Yorkshire Information Service
The North East Yorkshire Information Service (NEYIS) was a new project, created in response to the NDIP call for applications. Existing provision within North East Yorkshire was not strong. There was a disabled people's action group in Scarborough, a CAB covering Ryedale, Scarborough and Whitby and an active voluntary action group in Ryedale but few other providers of disability advice. The intention, therefore, was to establish a network of providers and to support them through the provision of information and other services.

Aims
The formal aims of the North East Yorkshire Information Service were:

• To establish a network of providers with access to a source of quality information whose members adhere to a minimum standard of service delivery.

• To unite existing providers to ensure that there is effective liaison and to avoid duplication.

- To improve access to information across the geographical area particularly in rural communities and those areas which do not currently have formal sources of information.

- To achieve user participation in the provision of information at all levels of the organisation.

Main characteristics

The structure and nature of NEYIS has been greatly influenced by geography. North East Yorkshire is a large and relatively sparsely populated area. The largest town is Scarborough on the coast at the south-eastern end of the district. The other, smaller town, Whitby, is also on the coast some 20 miles north of Scarborough. The North York Moors then stretch away to the west for about 30 or 40 miles. Here, in Ryedale, the population is very sparse and activities tend to focus on the small market towns and villages like Malton, Norton, Pickering and Kirkbymoorside on the southern edge of the moor. There are thus two focal points – Scarborough and Whitby – and a very large rural hinterland of Ryedale. These geographical characteristics were to play a major part in shaping the development of the project.

The initial work of the project involved attempts to identify needs and to develop ways of meeting them. Some research was undertaken but it failed to generate much in the way of useable results. Work in Scarborough tended to focus on the Disablement Action Group and on the development of a collection of documentary information and the development of a local database.

In Whitby some work was carried out with the local health authority developing information materials for disabled people and their carers. The project was also instrumental in developing the Whitby Disablement Action Group.

In Ryedale work was undertaken jointly with a carers' project based at the Family Health Services Authority. Information materials were prepared, based on the database developed in Scarborough and were made available through a town information centre and through GP surgeries.

Problems with staffing and project management absorbed a considerable amount of time and effort in the first couple of years of the project. It began to emerge, however, that the main problems were geographical. Put simply, North East Yorkshire was not a homogeneous area that could be covered by one small project. Accordingly, the project was effectively separated into three parts – one based in Scarborough, one in Whitby and one in Ryedale. In practice this appears to have relieved many of the previous tensions and the pace of the development work has accelerated.

The future

Within North East Yorkshire the disability information and advice work will, in future, be incorporated into activities of the three disability action groups, although in Ryedale the disability group has contracted with the local CAB to provide the service. Two of the groups have secured short-term financial support and the third continues to explore possibilities. One of the difficulties they face, however, arises from the fact that the level of support provided by NDIP was considered to be greatly in excess of what would normally be made available locally. There has been, therefore, a need to scale down expectations considerably.

Assessment

A number of issues emerge from the NEYIS experience. Probably the most important is the need to take account of geographical, social and local political factors when planning projects. It is better to work with the grain rather than against it.

The project also points to the difficulty of building a federation when existing levels of service provision are low. The overhead cost of a central servicing unit only becomes tolerable when the groups that are being supported are strong enough to pay the price.

There may be circumstances when an injection of resources from outside, as was the case with NDIP, enables a central unit to develop the network of service providers that it then goes on to support – this is what happened in Kent, for example. Once established, the network then becomes strong enough to take on the central overhead cost or recognises that the value added by the central unit to the services offered locally justifies the expense. This does, however, become something of a race against time: the central unit has two or three years to create the network that will provide its future support. If anything goes wrong, then at the end of the period of developmental funding, the whole superstructure will tend to collapse.

In North East Yorkshire a number of factors constrained the ability of the project to take off. They were to do with geography and local politics; with staffing and management problems; with the lack of a strong infrastructure to support the development and a lack of the other necessary ingredient – good luck.

Oldham Disability Alliance

Oldham Disability Alliance (ODA) was established with funding from NDIP. The application was submitted by the local DIAL, the CAB, and the local authority and was actively supported by 34 statutory and voluntary sector organisations. The project was intended to improve the delivery and coordination of information and advice services in Oldham, to explore a number of new approaches to work with the borough's minority ethnic communities, and to explore the use of the local authority housing benefit databases for targeting information.

Aims

ODA has three aims:

• To develop effective inter-agency cooperation.

• To identify shortfalls in information service provision.

• To share information, resources and expertise and through that to improve service delivery and inform policy development.

ODA encountered a number of difficulties in establishing clear aims and objectives. The grant awarded under NDIP was a great deal less than had originally been requested. It was not easy to scale down the aims of the project to fit the resources available. The management committee was undecided about whether the Alliance should provide a direct information service or support to providers but after some discussion, it was decided that ODA should be a back-up agency.

Main characteristics

ODA's work is both supportive and developmental. It has established a number of services to members and existing information providers in the borough. It has also completed several pieces of consultative development work including work with minority ethnic communities, and with people with learning disabilities. In all its development work ODA ensures active participation by disabled people, in order to understand needs and work towards meeting them.

The Alliance has improved the coordination of information provision and access to information in different ways. It has coordinated a number of events: bi-monthly meetings of information providers, information exhibitions in the town centre and a mobile exhibition using Action for Blind People's information bus.

ODA has produced and updated an *Information pack* (Oldham Disability Alliance, 1993b) for front-line workers and is about to publish a

Carers' information pack (Oldham Disability Alliance, 1994a) as well. A considerable amount of work has gone into producing the packs and the work has also been a valuable developmental exercise, raising ODA's profile in Oldham. It has also enabled ODA to become more familiar with local needs.

The information packs have been based on information held in a database devised by one of the project workers. This database has since been developed so that it can be made more widely available in the borough.

One of the main projects undertaken by the Alliance was the work with minority ethnic communities. It is often difficult to obtain feedback from different ethnic groups and they found that a consultative and cooperative approach was the only way to identify needs effectively and devise strategies for meeting them. The process proved to be time-consuming but essential (Oldham Disability Alliance, 1994c).

The Alliance has established a working group of people with learning disabilities. This aims to identify ways of improving access to information.

ODA commissioned research from Oxford University to investigate the information needs of disabled people. A second study looked at the needs of carers. The research took far longer than planned and the results are more limited than was hoped but every attempt has been made to use the results effectively (Oldham Disability Alliance, 1993a and 1994b). ODA organised a seminar with senior policy makers in the borough to discuss recommendations and how to implement them.

The future

ODA has become well-established within Oldham and benefits from considerable support from the local authority. The project has been assured of sufficient funding from the local authority to enable it to continue at much the same level as they experience during NDIP.

They plan to move into new premises with other disability organisations, including Oldham DIAL.

Assessment

ODA has a record of positive achievements and, after a difficult initial period, the project has achieved its objectives. The work with the black and ethnic minority community has opened up communication channels that did not previously exist and the exhibitions and meetings have done much to raise awareness of disability in the town. The information pack is a useful tool for professionals.

It must be recognised, however, that ODA received the largest of the grants from NDIP – the grant for 1993-94 was over £80,000 – and again there must be a question about whether, in terms of improving information and advice services to disabled people, the return on this expenditure was greater than it would have been had the money been spent on direct service provision.

The issue is the difficult one of weighing the balance of benefits between allocating resources to direct service provision and allocating them to activities that will have a less tangible return. It may have been the case in Oldham that sufficient resources were already allocated to direct advice provision – through the CAB and the DIAL – and it was therefore justifiable to allocate resources to the kind of activities undertaken by ODA.

Southwark Inform

The Southwark project began as the Southwark Disability Information Project, established jointly by the Southwark Disablement Association (SDA) and Southwark Consortium. Each of these organisations represent a range of groups from both the voluntary and statutory sectors, with SDA representing groups focused on physical disability, and Southwark Consortium representing groups working with people with learning difficulties.

The original intention was to build on SDA's information work and to create a centralised federation with a single enquiry point providing information and with federation members ensuring that the service met local needs. It soon became apparent that this approach was not working well and a decision was taken to concentrate on the other two aspects of the project: research into ways of meeting the information needs of people with learning difficulties and development work with disabled people from black and ethnic minority communities.

Aims

The original project had three aims:

- To improve access to information for disabled people who were isolated from any formal networks.

- To explore ways of making information accessible to people with learning difficulties.

- To improve access to information for disabled people from black and ethnic minority communities in Southwark.

After the first year, when the project was split, the first aim remained with SDA which subsequently withdrew from NDIP, and the others formed the basis for Southwark Inform, managed by the Southwark Consortium.

The project thus became much more like a fixed-term action research project that did not correspond to any of the federation models.

Main characteristics

The investigation of information provision for people with learning difficulties had two main strands: first, the development and testing of different means of providing information to people with learning difficulties; and second, the dissemination of good practice and cooperation throughout Southwark.

The project developed the use of Rebus and Makaton symbols and encouraged their use in Southwark as part of a commitment to *Total communication* – promoting much better communication with people with learning difficulties.

Southwark Inform experimented with the use of audiotape – for a directory of local services – still photography, video and posters. Each approach was tested by working with local groups of people with learning difficulties. All the products were evaluated (Moffatt, 1994). In addition, the project published reports on the provision of information for people with learning difficulties (Moffatt, 1993a and b). The reports are based on discussions held with both users and providers.

Other work involved trying to influence local statutory services in making information more accessible.

The work with disabled people from ethnic minorities was mainly concerned with making existing minority ethnic community groups aware of the problems and needs of disabled people. This involved a considerable amount of liaison and discussion, the results of which are presented in a report (Lomax, Steele and Telesford, 1994). The focus on women and health was felt to be appropriate as many of the ethnic minority groups contacted do not make a distinction between disability and health issues, and because women are traditionally more concerned than are men with health issues.

As with the work with people with learning difficulties, the ethnic minority work involved the development of a range of products. An example is *Health for You*, a package of information resources on women's alternative health care, aimed at people from ethnic minority communities. This was launched at a well-attended Health for You Day in June 1993 (Lomax, Steele and Telesford, 1994). Other products include a video on access to alternative healthcare for Asian women, and a poster project.

The future
Southwark Inform was planned as a pair of research projects that would come to an end at the conclusion of NDIP. It is to be hoped that the lessons learned will be incorporated into local practice in Southwark.

Assessment
This project pulled itself out of a difficult situation to achieve some worthwhile results. In part this can be attributed to the fact that, following the split, a realistic set of objectives were established, given the resources available. It must also be recognised that the character and achievements of the two strands of the project owe a great deal to the personality and persistence of the two staff involved. In any development work of this kind, personality factors are very significant determinants of success.

By the end of the three years the project had made a significant impact in Southwark. It also produced results that will be of much wider applicability.

Walsall Information Federation
The provision of information for disabled people in Walsall was poorly developed. There were no information or advice services specifically attempting to meet the needs of disabled people and there appeared to be a general lack of awareness that there was a problem. It was to overcome these barriers that Disability West Midlands and Walsall Borough Council took the lead in putting a bid together.

Rather than develop direct service provision, the project sought to raise awareness and generally promote better provision of information for disabled people. It had a particular focus on people from minority ethnic communities.

Aims
The Walsall Information Federation (WIF) had four aims:

- To improve the quality and accessibility of information services for disabled people, carers, enablers and service providers in Walsall.

- To enable information service users to influence and shape information services.

- To ensure that the specific information needs of disabled people from ethnic minority communities are met.

- To prevent duplication of information provision through a consistent coordinated approach which recognises the value of diversity, but avoids unnecessary fragmentation.

Main characteristics
The project was another that was slow to get off the ground because of staffing problems and difficulties with accommodation. For a major part of the three years WIF has operated with less than a full complement of staff. Certain changes to streamline the management committee structure also had to be made after the first year.

To help make up ground lost through staffing difficulties, WIF commissioned research to help them identify needs and priorities for development. This provided a basis from which to develop a longer term strategy.

In June 1993 WIF organised a Disability Information Day. The day provided WIF with 150 new members; it improved people's knowledge of information provision in Walsall; and generated a wide range of contacts with which to begin addressing some of the needs identified. It also helped to confirm some of WIF's perceptions of disability awareness in Walsall (Walsall Information Federation, 1993).

WIF established two user groups: one for users of disability information and one concerned specifically with the needs of black and Asian disabled people. To support the black and Asian disability group, WIF produced a guide to nationally available disability information in the main Asian languages (Walsall Information Federation, 1994a). Both user groups aim to establish a forum for consultation between WIF and disabled people, to promote awareness of WIF and to act as a link in the communication channel between users and information providers within three task groups.

These task groups of information providers have been established for the local authority; for the voluntary sector; and for the health services. The groups assess and review the ways in which they currently provide information for disabled people or about disability, and consider how they can make improvements and inform local policy. Arising partly from this discussion, WIF has produced a code of practice for information providers (Walsall Information Federation, 1994b).

A range of other services have been developed. These include a regular newsletter, disability equality training, quarterly meetings and a multi-lingual software resource.

The future
Despite these achievements, WIF was unable to secure long-term financial support and, as a consequence, the project was closed at the end of NDIP.

Assessment
As in North East Yorkshire, WIF has faced a major task in promoting development from a very low starting point. The process was hampered in the early stages by staff shortages and by management difficulties, particularly the complexities associated by joint management between the local authority and Disability West Midlands.

A considerable amount has been achieved. The code of practice, the user groups and the task forces together provide a platform from which improved information provision can be developed. A great deal, however, remains to be done. There is almost certainly a need for an effective public access disability information and advice service in Walsall. The creation of such a service would be the next logical step in the development of provision of information services for disabled people. Yet the project has not had long enough at full strength to develop the momentum required.

The achievements of the pilot projects
It should be stressed that the purpose of the pilot projects within the National Disability Information Project was to test different ways of developing information and advice services for disabled people. Each was treading new ground with no guarantees of success. Indeed, the essence of the project was to enable local groups to take risks that would be difficult to justify to other funders. NDIP was, above all else, a means of accelerating the process of trial and error.

The achievements of the pilot projects need to be looked at in this context. It has frequently been the case that project staff and their management committees have grappled with difficulties that were not always of their own making and, despite all their best efforts, have been forced to conclude that the task that was set them was impossible to achieve.

In many of the projects it is possible to point to very tangible successes. In some others, unforeseen circumstances, often associated with staff shortages, have tipped the balance and have made it difficult to achieve the results that were hoped for. In yet other cases, structural and unavoidable problems – like the geography of North East Yorkshire – have forced projects to re-assess their aims and to re-structure their activities.

Certain general lessons can be drawn from the experience – further, more particular lessons will be discussed in Parts Three and Four of the book. First, it is apparent that the time and effort expended on the compilation of a database of information about local services and organisations is seldom justified. The creation of such databases absorbs a considerable amount of staff resources: the cost in one of the NDIP pilot projects was assessed at over £50,000. Having established the database it then needs to be kept up to date and this is also time-consuming. If the effort were put into direct service provision, the return, in the form of improved information and advice services for disabled people could be greater.

That is not necessarily to say that information and advice services can be provided without having access to reliable sources of information. Rather, it suggests that the decision to compile a database should follow from a careful analysis of the need for information. In many cases the most pressing need felt by advice workers is for support in dealing with matters like benefit or housing problems. This calls for access to nationally produced information sources like the *Disability rights handbook*. In such circumstances, the existence of a database of local information is of limited value.

The position has changed considerably during NDIP. There are now a number of commercially available databases that can provide much of the information needed by a local service. It may well be more cost-effective to buy one of these database packages, and the updating service that goes with it, than to develop something locally.

In many cases it is more cost-effective to collect information when it is needed than it is to collect it in anticipation of a potential need arising in the future. Here, economies of scale clearly come into play. If a database has a significant number of active users then the cost of collection may well be justified by the volume of use made of the information.

Secondly, there is no real substitute for direct provision of information and advice services. Information comes best when wrapped in a person. Just about all of us, when faced with a problem, a need to find something out or a desire to make use of a service, want to talk to another person – someone who can provide the information, advice and assistance that we require; someone who can tailor that information and advice to our particular circumstances; someone who can advise on the best course of action. It may be that the advice is reinforced with printed, Brailled, or taped information but information alone is seldom enough. Where projects have not worked closely with direct providers of information and advice – often because they did not exist – then the impact of their work appears to have been limited.

Thirdly, multi-agency working is time-consuming and complex. This is particularly the case when seeking to reconcile the different cultures of the statutory and voluntary sectors. Constitutional, political and management problems have absorbed considerable amounts of time and energy in many of the NDIP projects as they have in most voluntary sector projects. The scale of the problem appears to grow exponentially in proportion to the number and diversity of organisations involved in the management of the projects.

Finally, there is the relationship between central support services and the local agencies that benefit from them. Two types of relationship between the central unit and the local services emerged from NDIP. The central unit can act in a community development role, assisting local services to become established, as happened in Kent. Or the central unit can provide a range of services – training, information, tribunal representation, for example – to support the work of local information and advice services. It has become clear from the work of some of the pilot projects that these community development and support service roles are very different, calling for different skills and strategies.

Where few local disability information and advice services exist, then the main task of the central unit is to create the conditions in which local services might develop. This is what happened in Kent and, towards the end of the project in the Whitby and Ryedale areas of North East Yorkshire. Only when the local services are operating at a reasonable level does it become feasible to provide support in the form of training programmes or local databases.

In areas where the basic framework of local services has become established, it is feasible to provide support services. Indeed, it is a very cost-effective way of proceeding as it enables all services to take advantage of economies of scale and the other benefits that can result from collaboration. It is clear that it is easier to add value to well-established services than to services that are in the early stages of development.

When developing the aims, objectives and strategy for a federation, it is therefore, crucially important to be clear about the state of development of the local services that the organisation seeks to federate and to plan accordingly.

It is also necessary to understand that well-established local services will, quite rightly, perceive any central support unit to be an overhead on their business. And overheads of that kind are only justifiable if the cost is less than the value added. More precisely, the overhead is only justified if the value added by the central unit is greater than the value that would be added if the financial resources committed to that central unit were instead distributed to the local services. The message here is that if the local services, or beneficiaries, are not convinced that the central unit represents good value for money, then maybe it would be better to consider a re-allocation of the resources.

We shall return to these and other issues to emerge from the work of the pilot projects in Part Four.

References

Devon Disability Information and Advice Federation (1994a) *Can we help you? A video-based training resource*

Devon Disability Information and Advice Federation (1994b) *Keyword classification scheme*

Devon Disability Information and Advice Federation (1994c) *Stepping stones to quality*

Gateshead Disability Information Project (1993a) *Gateshead directory of support and self-help groups*

Gateshead Disability Information Project (1993b) *Into work: an employment guide for disabled people (CD-i)*

Gateshead Disability Information Project (1993c) *Into work: an evaluation report*

Gateshead Disability Information Project (1994a) *Gateshead black and ethnic minority resource directory*

Gateshead Disability Information Project (1994b) *Gateshead disability information pack*

Gateshead Disability Information Project (1994c) *Guide to Gateshead hospitals (CD-i)*

Gateshead Disability Information Project (1994d) *Tyneside directory of self-help and support groups*

GUIDE (1993) *Thesaurus of disability terms*

GUIDE (1994) *GUIDE information system*

Lomax, Julie, Steele, Andre and Telesford, Jimmy (1994) *Voices*. Southwark Inform

Marsh, Linda (1994) *Break IT: an examination of access for disabled people to information via information technology*. Manchester Disability Information Service

Moffatt, Virginia (1993a) *Keep it simple! A guide to creating accessible documents*. Southwark Inform

Moffatt, Virginia (1993b) *The right to know: informing people with learning difficulties – some issues and problems*. Southwark Inform

Moffatt, Virginia (1994) *What's the point of writing when I don't know how to read? Using different media to inform people with learning difficulties*. Southwark Inform

Norfolk Disability Information Federation (1994a) *A guide to services in Norfolk for visually impaired people*

Norfolk Disability Information Federation (1994b) *Guidelines on information for sensorily-impaired people*

Norfolk Disability Information Federation (1994c) *Putting information on the map*

Oldham Disability Alliance (1993a) *Carers' information survey*

Oldham Disability Alliance (1993b) *Information pack*

Oldham Disability Alliance (1994a) *Carers' information pack*

Oldham Disability Alliance (1994b) *Information needs of disabled people*

Oldham Disability Alliance (1994c) *Making contact*

Simpkins, Rebecca (1993) *Planning and evaluating disability information services.* Policy Studies Institute

Walsall Information Federation (1993) *Walsall disability information day: a review*

Walsall Information Federation (1994a) *Disability information guide: disability information available in Asian languages*

Walsall Information Federation (1994b) *Information provision for people with disabilities: a code of practice*

6   The project team

The project team was selected at the same time as the 12 pilot projects. Out of six organisations that were invited to tender for the work, the Department chose the Policy Studies Institute (PSI). The Institute is one of Britain's leading social research organisations, undertaking studies of economic, industrial and social policy. PSI is a registered charity and is not associated with any political party, pressure group or commercial interest.

In 1989 PSI established a group to undertake research into the policy issues that were raised by information and its use in society. The staff who formed the NDIP project team were drawn from this Information Policy Group.

Purpose and limitations

The overall purpose of the project team was to undertake the management of NDIP on behalf of the Department. It was to provide advice and support to the local pilot projects; to monitor and review progress; to disseminate the lessons learned in the project and provide a framework for future development. It was also to work with national information providers.

From the outset, it was clear that the project team would have to work within certain limitations. First, we were not in a position to manage the pilot projects. Even if we had wished to do so, there would not have been sufficient resources – the contract from the Department provided for the equivalent of 3.75 full-time staff. Each of the pilot projects was anyway constituted as an autonomous organisation, accountable to the Department of Health for the expenditure of the NDIP grant, but accountable also to the local community that they had been established to serve.

It was important that this autonomy and local accountability were not jeopardised by their participation in NDIP. Without them the value of the lessons that would be learned would be diminished. The conditions under which the projects operated were already unusual – few voluntary sector projects, for example, have the luxury of budgets that are, more or less, assured for three years – and it was important not to introduce further external factors that would distort the real local circumstances.

Any advice and support provided by the project team had, therefore, to be offered carefully and sensitively so as to keep the experience as real as possible. On occasions it was necessary to step back from intervening in a local project when it seemed to us that something was going wrong. On other occasions it was appropriate to raise questions and suggest courses of action in the knowledge that the final decision had to rest locally. This was one of the most difficult aspects of the work. Resisting the temptation to intervene was seldom easy.

We also had to recognise that, while the original brief stated that the project team was 'to coordinate initiatives with national information providers' they too were autonomous organisations that did not take kindly to the notion that they might be coordinated by the project team. Promoting cooperation is one thing, but coordination implies having an ability to instruct or to coerce those organisations that are to be coordinated. Clearly the project team was not in a position to do this. The best we could hope for was to work with the national information providers, encouraging them to adopt a cooperative approach to the issues that faced them. But if any chose not to cooperate, then there was little we could do about it.

In short, we had to work with people and organisations. We were not in a position to direct them.

Advice and support

One of the main functions of the project team was to provide the local pilot projects with advice and support. As we have noted, it was important to ensure that advice and support did not become interference, back-seat management or an attempt to impose control from London.

We sought to provide advice directly to the pilot projects as they requested it. We also tried to share the lessons among the pilot projects. To achieve this we nominated, from among the members of the project team, a contact person for each pilot project; we held regular quarterly meetings of all the pilot projects; we produced a current awareness bulletin; we provided some training and we provided specific support on computing matters.

The system of contact officers for each pilot seemed to work well. Each research fellow on the project team was allocated four pilot projects and, as far as was possible, they maintained their link with these projects through the life of NDIP. They made regular visits to the pilots and were the first point of contact if anyone in a pilot project had an enquiry or a request for specific assistance.

The quarterly meetings of the pilot projects also provided a useful opportunity to exchange experience, to bring each other up to date with developments and to discuss common problems. Even though the meetings were big – often there were more than 30 participants – and were not always attended by the same people, a common identity did emerge even if, on occasion, it was stimulated by a desire to point out to the project team the error of its ways.

The *Current Awareness Bulletin* (Johnson, 1991-94) was intended to provide the pilot projects with up-to-date information about general developments in the provision of information and advice for disabled people. The rationale was that if this function was undertaken by the project team, it would save the pilot projects a great deal of time and effort in keeping themselves in touch with developments. The *Bulletin* proved to be very successful and, in response to an obvious demand, it was made more widely available on subscription.

The project team initially had plans to develop a range of training events for the pilot projects. In the event, it became clear that much of the demand for training could best be met locally with the pilot projects taking advantage of training courses offered by organisations like councils for voluntary service. To assist this process, the project team circulated information about such training provision.

The team did provide some training. Courses were organised on publicity and promotion, writing skills, the costing of work and information systems.

Computer support was provided by the Computer Development Unit (CDU) of the London Advice Services Alliance, working under a sub-contract from the project team. CDU was selected because it had a great deal of experience of working with local information and advice services, advising and supporting them on their use of information technology. CDU's first task was to visit each pilot project to advise the Department on the capital equipment requirements. Some projects had included extensive bids for capital equipment in their initial applications, others had made very little provision and it was thought to be sensible to take an overall view and to explore the scope and need for standardisation of equipment.

CDU was retained to provide support throughout the life of NDIP. The staff were available to advise pilot projects facing particular difficulties. They provided two residential training courses on the use and development of databases and information systems. They also developed a basic mailing list system that pilot projects could use as a foundation for their information systems development.

It became clear that there was a demand, both within the pilot projects and more generally, for a very basic information management system that could be used by local disability information and advice services. CDU was therefore commissioned to build on their earlier work and to develop a cheap and robust system that could be made widely available.

It also became clear that there was a demand for a classification scheme that could be used to organise information materials in local disability information and advice centres. A number of such schemes had been developed. The one that was by far the most commonly used was the scheme developed by the Disability Information Service in Surrey (DISS). We commissioned the University of Central England to review the use made of this scheme and to explore the scope for developing it for use in a wide range of services (Nankivell and Brown, 1994).

The other area of support provided by the project team concerned the financial arrangements for the projects. The contractual arrangement was clearly between the Department of Health and each pilot project. Within that arrangement, there was a need for the project team to assist both the Department and the pilot projects with the process of financial administration. This principally involved collecting information about past and planned expenditure so that the Department could adjust the allocation of its resources, taking account of any underspends at the end of the financial year.

Monitoring and review

The work of the project team demanded more than an uncritical acceptance of the work conducted by the pilot projects. The team was required to monitor progress and report on this to the steering group and to the Department. The process of monitoring and review was also important as a basis for developing an understanding of the problems faced by the pilot projects, the strategies that were developed to overcome the problems and the lessons that could be learned.

It was also important to ensure that each of the pilot projects undertook their own monitoring and evaluation. Most had included plans for self-evaluation in their applications. Others developed their approaches as the projects proceeded. It was, however, thought to be useful for the project team to codify the experience of the pilot projects and others and to produce a set of guidelines that could be used more widely (Simpkins, 1993).

Finally, it was necessary to ensure that the monitoring and review process fitted in with the overall evaluation work that was being undertaken by the team from RICA.

The principal mechanism for reviewing the projects was a series of six-monthly meetings between members of the project team and each pilot project. The purpose of these meetings was twofold. First they provided the pilot projects with an opportunity to take stock of what had been happening, to assess the development that had taken place and to revise plans for the future. For the project team they provided a series of opportunities to get to know the workings of the projects, to monitor and review progress, to draw out lessons that might be of more general application and to promote the sharing of information among members of the pilot project network.

Before each review meeting, the pilot projects were asked to produce a short report reviewing progress since the last meeting, noting any changes in aims and objectives that were required in the light of that progress and setting out the plans and targets for the next six months. This report then formed the basis for the review meeting. After the meeting the project team produced a formal response to the pilot projects, summing up the discussions. Copies of both reports were made available to the Department.

The meetings were attended by project staff and by members of the management committees. They provided a valuable opportunity to raise issues and to discuss tactics and strategy. They were particularly important given the limitations on time within which the projects were operating. It would have been very easy for time to slip by and for the projects to find that they were approaching the end of NDIP without having done all they set out to do. By holding regular six-monthly reviews it was possible in some cases to identify problems early on and to modify plans accordingly. In other cases, the intervention of the project team – a group that was distanced from the day-to-day concerns of the pilot – made it easier to confront difficulties and obstacles. In yet other cases, the project team was able to raise issues that would have been difficult for either the management committee or the pilot project staff to raise.

The need for a set of guidelines on project planning, monitoring and evaluation became apparent at an early stage. This form of monitoring and evaluation should be part and parcel of management in the voluntary sector. It is clear, however, that this is far from the case and the NDIP pilot projects were, in this respect, no different from other voluntary sector organisations. Some had well-defined evaluation strategies, others were learning as they went along.

The two objectives of the guidelines were 'to define and describe the processes of planning and evaluating services and to provide practical guidance on how these processes can be applied'. Wherever possible, they drew on the experience of the pilot projects. The projects in Devon, Kent and Norfolk, in particular, provided practical help and guidance.

The project team was also required to consider overall approaches to the quality of disability information provision. The specification for the work stated that the team was:

> To develop national standards of quality control of disability information services, reflecting the totality of features and characteristics of the service that bear on its ability to satisfy stated or implied needs.

At the time when NDIP was launched there was considerable enthusiasm for the quality approach that had been developed by the British Standards Institution and published as BS 5750, along with the comparable international standard ISO 9000. This standard had been developed in the context of manufacturing industry and organisations in the service sector were beginning to apply it. It was thought that it would provide a useful tool for information services concerned with quality assurance.

In December 1991 the International Standards Organisation was due to publish ISO 10004 – *Quality systems: a guide to quality management for services* – and the project team planned to use this as the basis for developing a quality assurance framework for disability information.

In the event, the publication was delayed and has since been shelved indefinitely. What is more, the approach embodied in BS 5750 has increasingly been called into question. There are two main reasons for this. The first is that it is a very cumbersome technique that requires a great deal of documentation of processes and procedures. It is also quite expensive. For relatively large-scale manufacturing concerns the scale and cost may well be justifiable. For organisations in the service sector, the case is much less clear-cut.

The second cause of the doubts about BS 5750 concerns the fact that all it does is state that the organisation concerned has conformed to the quality standards that it specified for itself and that the procedures for monitoring this are working effectively. Where it is difficult to specify outputs – and this is especially difficult for information and advice services – it is difficult to specify meaningful quality standards.

In short, during the life of NDIP, BS 5750 began to go out of fashion. It did not seem to be worth using it as the basis for what was intended as a national quality framework. Instead, a better approach seemed to be through ensuring that local projects set realistic objectives for themselves, that they monitored their activities and assessed regularly whether or not they were achieving their objectives. This was the approach embodied in the planning and evaluation guidelines. At a national level, the opportunity was taken to explore the issue in some depth in a working party of representatives of national information providers. The results of this consideration are contained in the report of the working party (National Disability Information Project, 1994). This work is described in greater detail below.

Dissemination and support for future development
From the outset it was recognised that NDIP was not operating in isolation. In addition to those working in the pilot projects there were many others who were actively involved in the development of information and advice services for disabled people. It would not have been sensible to expect these other people to suspend development for three years to await the results of the project. Instead, an active attempt was made to ensure that there was a consistent and effective flow of information throughout the life of the project.

We adopted three main approaches. First we tried to ensure that there was a regular flow of news about developments in the pilot projects and elsewhere. This was achieved through the *NDIP Newsletter*. Secondly we tried to produce practical guidance on a range of issues that were of general concern. And thirdly, we tried to stimulate the exchange of information through the annual conferences and by putting organisations in touch with one another.

The *NDIP Newsletter* proved to one of the most tangible successes of the project. The main aim was to create a vehicle that could be used to keep a large number of people and organisations informed about what was happening within NDIP but also to provide news and information about developments generally (Mason, 1991-94).

The original expectation was that the circulation for the *Newsletter* would steadily build up to a distribution of about 1,000. This was exceeded with the first issue and, by the end of the first year the circulation had risen to over 6,000. The *Newsletter* was free and available on demand. It was also distributed through a number of relevant networks – the National Association of Citizens Advice Bureaux, for example, distributed it to all their bureaux.

The first set of guidelines we produced discussed the concept of disability information federations (Simpkins and Nadash, 1993). There was clearly a considerable degree of confusion about what constituted a disability information federation. As we have seen, the Coopers and Lybrand report failed to provide a definition, recommending instead that 'immediate steps should be taken to define the concept in more detail' (Coopers and Lybrand, 1988). There was also considerable interest in what had happened to the federations that had been unsuccessful in their application to become NDIP projects.

We attempted to trace the unsuccessful applicants. Of the 95 federations contacted, 71 responded. Only 29 of the 71 were still in operation as disability information federations and, of these, 26 had been successful in obtaining funding. Based on the analysis of these surviving federations and the pilot projects, it was possible to identify three broad types of service:

- Direct information provision to the public.

- The development of resources, such as local databases, which are made available to the public through other member organisations.

- Development work, along with the support and coordination of disability information services in the locality.

Most federations appeared to concentrate on the provision of support and coordination to disability information providers.

The guidelines provided a useful analytical framework within which it has been possible to consider the work undertaken by the pilot projects and others.

The next pressing issue concerned the funding of disability information services. The pilot projects were beginning to draw up their plans for long-term funding and financial support was clearly a problem that faced many other local disability information and advice providers.

The funding guidelines (Shiner, 1993) had two main purposes. First, to provide practical assistance with the fundraising process and secondly, to review the different sources of finance that were open to disability information and advice services. The guidelines drew particularly on the experience of the pilot projects in Birmingham, Devon, Gloucestershire and Kent and the Disability Information Service in Hertfordshire.

The main conclusion to come from the guidelines was that the principal source of finance was local authorities, followed by health authorities. Most other sources were tenuous. Private sector finance was insignificant.

We have already discussed the guidelines on planning and evaluation (Simpkins, 1993).

Two other areas of work presented pilot projects with particular difficulties: research into the information needs of disabled people and the development of local directories and databases. We decided to make both the subject of guidelines.

The guidance on researching disability information needs drew on the experience of pilot projects like Birmingham, Oldham and Walsall that had commissioned outside organisations to carry out research on behalf of the project and pilots like Manchester that had undertaken the work themselves (Simpkins, 1994).

The guidelines discuss the difficulties of conducting research in this area. It is notoriously difficult to conduct research to explore people's information needs – most of us do not realise we have a need for information until it is realised. The guidelines provide practical recommendations for ways in which the problems can be overcome. They also include guidance on how to work with an external research agency.

We have seen that many of the pilot projects developed directories and databases of local information. In nearly every case this process was fraught with difficulties and, again in most cases, the task took much longer than expected. The guidelines are an attempt to distil the lessons from this experience (Rooney and Shiner, 1995). They draw on a wide range of experience, particularly in the pilot projects that had given priority to the development of databases, such as Berkshire, Devon, Gloucestershire, Kent, Norfolk and Oldham. They analyse all the steps that should be taken to decide whether or not a database is needed, what form it might take and how it might be constructed. The guidelines also review the different proprietary systems that are commercially available.

These guidelines should help a wide range of organisations build on the experience of the NDIP projects, avoiding some of the errors and benefiting from the successes.

In addition to the formal guidance, there was a need to stimulate the general exchange of information through the system. In many respects, the best way to learn is through direct contact with a similar organisation. For this reason and to give us an idea of the overall pattern of local disability information and advice provision, we compiled a directory of local information providers (Nadash, 1993). An additional benefit of the directory was that it provided national information providers with a mailing list that they could use to make contact with local services.

The directory proved to be a much larger task than we expected. No-one knew how many local services there were in operation. Some thought that there were as many as 250, others thought that this was an over-estimate. We therefore sent questionnaires to as many potential organisations as possible, drawing on the *Newsletter* mailing list and working with the cooperation of social services departments, national organisations and others concerned with disability or information provision.

Clearly disability information is available from many sources – ranging from social services departments through CABx to local disability action groups. The directory was restricted to groups that could provide information on a wide range of disability issues or that focused on information that was likely to be relevant to most disabled people. Entries were also restricted to groups that had information and advice provision as their main, or one of their main objectives. This usually meant that they had staff dedicated to the collection and provision of information and that they advertised themselves as an information and advice service. On the basis of these criteria we identified over 600 organisations that could justifiably be described as local providers of information and advice for disabled people.

The final element in the strategy to communicate the results of NDIP is this book, which attempts to draw out the overall lessons and to bring together all the various strands of development.

We have already noted that information comes best when wrapped in a person. We are, therefore, aware that written guidelines have their limitations. There is great value in providing people with opportunities to discuss issues and to exchange experience. The main mechanism for this has been the conferences that have been organised in conjunction with NDIP.

The first conference took place in the International Convention Centre in Birmingham in November 1991 and was an event to launch NDIP. The conference provided an opportunity for people generally to see what the newly selected pilot projects were offering and it began a process of information exchange among local groups.

A year later Britain held the Presidency of the European Community and, to mark the event, the Department of Health held a combined conference and exhibition entitled *Inform '92*. The aim was to discuss information provision for disabled people in a European context. A large number of organisations, including many of the pilot projects, took part in the exhibition and contributed papers to the conference (*Inform '92*, 1993).

Because *Inform '92* was held at the end of the first year of NDIP it did not seem sensible to hold a separate NDIP conference. Instead, this was deferred until April 1993 when a two-day residential conference, attended by over 300 people, was held at the University of Nottingham. This overcame some of the accommodation problems that were faced by people attending the conferences in Birmingham. It also meant that, as the conference accommodation was all on the same campus, it was much easier for people to continue discussion into the evening.

The conference appears to have been a great success. There was significant demand for written versions of the papers – so we decided to produce a set of the proceedings (*Information enables*, 1993). Many people commented on the value of the opportunity the conference presented to meet and talk to others who were facing similar problems in the development of their services.

A second conference was held in the same place in March 1994 and a third is planned for March 1995. It is to be hoped that these conferences can be continued. Many people developing disability information services are doing so in relative isolation, with very few spare resources available to cover the cost of visiting other similar services from which they might learn a great deal. The conferences provide an opportunity to make contacts and to find out at first hand what is going on.

The NDIP conferences have, however, focused attention on the pressing need for a residential conference venue that can meet the accommodation needs of disabled people. The University of Nottingham and the East Midlands Conference Centre are very cooperative, providing the best possible service within the limitations they face. And they are better than anywhere else in their price range, but the accommodation is still not really suitable for people with disabilities.

The process of dissemination has no end. No matter how much information is made available, there will always be people and groups who miss out, often because they are not part of any formal network. It is also necessary to relay information continuously to inform people who are new to the field or who missed out the first time around. Also, information needs to be updated constantly. It does, however, seem that a reasonable start has been made, and it is to be hoped that the *Newsletter* and the annual conferences can continue into the future.

National information providers

An important element in the pattern of disability information provision is the work of the national information providers. Much of the information that is used by local disability information services is best collected and processed nationally. The national information providers can take advantage of economies of scale and from the savings that result from the avoidance of duplication. The work with national information providers thus presented a significant part of the project team's activity.

The first task was to define what was meant by a national information provider. The Coopers and Lybrand report had talked of 'common service providers', other documents referred to 'common information providers'. Many organisations felt that they could be regarded as such. Our first task was to identify a group that had sufficient cohesion to enable them to work together.

Clearly a very large number of national organisations provide information that is of some use to disabled people. Within this overall group it is possible to identify three different categories:

- *National Disability Information Provider*
  They operate at a national level providing information that is aimed at all, or a large proportion of disabled people. They cover broad, general subjects like aids and equipment or benefits.

- *Specific Disability Information Provider*
  They also operate at a national level, providing information aimed at a more specific audience. These organisations cover subjects related to a specific disability or impairment, or a more specialised subject area, such as the use of computers for learners who have special educational needs.

- *Generalist Information Provider*
  These organisations provide information for general consumption. Some of the information will be concerned with disability issues.

Having drawn up this categorisation we discussed it with the Disability Information Coordination Committee. This group had arisen out of an earlier series of meetings that had been convened by the National Information Forum. The categorisation met with general approval.

Having defined and identified the national information providers, it became possible to establish and to explore the main policy issues faced by them. We were also able to produce a directory setting out information about their activities and the information services and products that they provide (Hinkley and Steele, 1992). This directory along with the discussion of policy issues was published as *National disability information provision: sources and issues.*

During 1992, a number of discussions were held in order to identify the most pressing issues facing these national information providers. The clear consensus to emerge from these discussions was that there were four main issues that needed to be considered:

- The funding and pricing of national disability information services and products.

- The quality of the information services and products and the need to develop effective approaches to quality assurances.

- Gaps and duplication in the provision of information.

- The application of information technology.

In late 1992 a series of open meetings, to which all the national information providers were invited, was called to discuss these issues. In the event, the size of the meetings and the disparities between the organisations made it difficult to get to grips with the issues and, as a consequence, it was decided instead to set up working groups with a more tightly defined remit and a pre-determined membership.

The first two working groups were established in 1993 to consider funding and pricing and the issues concerned with quality (National Disability Information Project, 1994).

The question of gaps and duplication was covered in part at least by a research study into the use of national disability information by local disability information and advice services. This study was carried out by Colin Barnes of the BCODP Research Unit at Leeds University (Barnes, 1994). The work is discussed in more detail below.

At an early stage it was decided that it was not sensible to consider information technology as a separate issue. There was a strong feeling that it should be considered as a factor affecting each of the other issues.

The overall aim of the funding and pricing working group was to identify and discuss the various issues concerned with the funding and pricing of national disability information services and products and to make whatever recommendations appeared to be appropriate. Within that broad aim the group had four specific objectives:

- To identify the respective roles of national and local information providers.

- To identify the size and characteristics of the different markets for disability information services and products.

- To explore the different options for funding national disability information provision.

- To explore the pricing of national information services and products, identifying the different pricing strategies that might be adopted by the national information providers.

The working party analysed the overall disability information system, concluding that there was an important role for both national and local information providers and that the relationship between the two should be strengthened. There was a clear case for central government to provide financial support for the work of national providers. The working party also considered the different pricing strategies that could be used to recover at least part of the information collection and processing cost from local services.

The overall aim of the working group on quality was to produce practical suggestions for national information providers on ways of improving and monitoring the quality of their services. Within this, the working party had the following objectives:

- To share information and experience and to consider models of good practice.

- To consider the needs of different groups of users.

- To suggest criteria for measuring the quality of a service and methods for improving quality and to consider the structures that will be needed post-NDIP.

The working party concluded that, while the variety of types of service offered by national information providers made it difficult to define and measure quality, it was possible to evolve a three-stage strategy. This requires the providers to establish the need of their users; to identify the components of a good quality service; and then take steps to implement improvements.

Following the initial meetings with the national information providers, it became clear that a number of them were unclear about the requirements of local disability information and advice services. It was equally clear from our other work that local services were equally uncertain about what it was that national information providers did.

To overcome the uncertainties a small exhibition was held in 1993 in which nearly all the national information providers participated. Representatives from local services found the exhibition very useful and there were plans to repeat the exercise in conjunction with the national conference. Unfortunately restrictions on space prevented this in 1993 and 1994, but the space problem should be overcome with the 1995 conference.

The relationship between national and local information providers was the subject of a research study. It was clear from our earlier discussions that the work needed to be undertaken. It was equally clear at the time that the project team was working to full capacity. Accordingly it was decided to sub-contract the work. A research specification was prepared and three organisations submitted proposals.

The contract was awarded to Dr Colin Barnes and the BCODP Research Unit at Leeds University. They carried out a postal survey backed up by face-to-face interviews to explore the extent to which local disability information and advice services made use of the information provided by national information providers.

The overall conclusions of the work were that there was a general lack of understanding. Local groups did not fully appreciate what was available from national information providers. At the same time, the national information providers were unaware of what the local services required (Barnes, 1994).

It is fair to say that we did not achieve as much as we expected in our work with the national information providers. In part this was simply because initial expectations were unrealistic. We have already commented on the impossibility of being able to coordinate otherwise autonomous organisations, particularly when they perceive themselves to be in competition for funding.

Equally, the early stages of the RICA evaluation found that some of the national information providers expected to receive some kind of additional financial support from NDIP and were rather disenchanted when this failed to materialise (Yelding, Rigg and More O'Ferrall, 1993).

The position is further complicated by the fact that the national providers do not constitute a homogeneous group. They differ markedly in size, financial resources and in the nature of the information services that they provide. This was brought home particularly clearly in the attempt to consider the information technology issues. Some organisations were very advanced in their use of information technology – the Disabled Living Foundation, for example, was experimenting with the use of compact discs for information storage – while another was unable to overcome the problems caused by the incompatibility of its two personal computers.

A significant amount of work is still needed to improve disability information provision at national level. The future is, however, bright. Despite all the financial and other problems that the national providers are facing, there is a good deal of common ground and a willingness to share information and experience. It is to be hoped that NDIP has started a ball rolling that will now gather its own momentum.

Project management

Within the limitations imposed by the need to preserve the autonomy of the pilot projects and the independence of the national information providers, the project team was responsible for keeping the whole NDIP process on track. This meant managing the day-to-day activities for which were we responsible and ensuring that everything kept to time and to budget. This work was undertaken within the general project management framework provided by the Policy Studies Institute.

Overall direction was provided by the project steering group. This was identified by the RICA evaluation as one of the less successful aspects of the project (Yelding, Rigg and More O'Ferrall, 1993).

A number of factors contributed to the fact that the steering group made less impact than it might have done. The members of the steering group were selected carefully by the Department of Health: they were to be people who had an interest in disability information but, it was decided, they should not be associated with organisations that might benefit from NDIP. While understandable, this logic for selection did not prove to be tenable. NDIP set out to be wide-ranging and to involve as many organisations as possible. The criterion therefore meant that the people who were selected, almost by definition, were people for whom disability information was not their first priority nor was it an area of particular experience or expertise. As a consequence, on the occasions when the inevitable pressures of busy lives forced them to decide whether or not to attend the NDIP steering group meetings, other calls on their time prevailed. In the latter part of the project, steps were taken to remedy this and people with more direct experience of information and advice work were invited to join the steering group.

The result was a series of meetings that were poorly attended. This led to a lack of continuity and to a situation where members, other than the small number who were able to attend most meetings, were not sufficiently well informed about the issues under discussion simply because they had been unable to attend previous meetings.

It also has to be recognised that NDIP was a complex project and it was difficult, even for the people who were involved full-time, to keep all the different elements in view.

Despite these reservations, the steering group has provided the project team with a useful regular opportunity to review progress, to consider and debate the issues, and to plan future development.

Post NDIP follow-up

It had always been recognised that NDIP would not fully achieve the objectives set at the beginning. As NDIP drew to a close, the nature of the additional work that was required to consolidate the gains that had been made became apparent. The clear priority was for work to support the emerging network of local disability information and advice services. Many of these were new and were developing in isolation. Yet they provided a vital link in the information chain and, if successfully developed, could make a very significant contribution.

Discussions among the pilot projects, at the NDIP conference, and more generally, stimulated by the *NDIP Newsletter* suggested that two main things were needed: local groups needed opportunities to share information and exchange experience; they also needed some mechanism to represent their interests at national level.

The discussions also revealed quite clearly that the existence of NDIP and the project team had filled a vacuum that had once existed and that at the end of the project the vacuum would reappear. It was, therefore, particularly important that the project team did not take a strong lead in stimulating post-NDIP developments. The risk that the initiative would falter when NDIP ended was simply too great. It was also important that any initiative should come from within the groups themselves. It was a time for accountability and for ownership.

Fortunately there was a widespread concern that development should not cease with the end of NDIP. In July 1994 DIAL UK convened a meeting of national information providers, networks representing local disability information and advice services, NDIP pilot projects and other interested parties to discuss whether or not something should be done to carry forward the NDIP initiative.

It was agreed at this meeting that there was virtue in trying to create a mechanism to take the work forward and that this should focus on continuing the *NDIP Newsletter* and the annual conference, and on securing funding to employ a development worker who could work with the networks and with individual services, representing their interests at national level and providing practical, developmental support.

The main networks of local services agreed to come together to form the Alliance of Disability Advice and Information Providers and to submit a bid under Section 64 for resources to cover this work. The outcome of the application is awaited with interest.

References

Barnes, Colin (1994) *From national to local: an evaluation of the effectiveness of national disablement information providers' services to local disablement information providers.* British Council of Organisations of Disabled People

Coopers and Lybrand (1988) *Information needs of disabled people, their carers and service providers.* Department of Health and Social Security

Hinkley and Steele (1992) *National disability information provision: sources and issues.* Policy Studies Institute

Inform '92: meeting the information needs of disabled people in Europe Department of Health (1993)

Information enables: improving access to information services for disabled people. Policy Studies Institute (1993)

Johnson, Susan (editor) (1991-94) *NDIP current awareness bulletin.* Policy Studies Institute, monthly

Mason, Sara (editor) (1991-94) *NDIP Newsletter.* Policy Studies Institute

Nadash, Pamela (1993) *Directory of local disability information providers.* Policy Studies Institute

Nankivell, Clare and Brown, Pauline (1994) *Can the DISS classification scheme be developed for national use?* University of Central England

National Disability Information Project (1994) *National disability information provision: the main issues.* Policy Studies Institute

Rooney, Michael and Shiner, Michael (1995) *Managing disability information: guidelines on directories and databases.* Policy Studies Institute

Shiner, Michael (1993) *Fundraising: sources and skills for disability information services.* Policy Studies Institute

Rebecca Simpkins (1994) *Guidelines on conducting research into the information needs of disabled people.* Policy Studies Institute

Simpkins, Rebecca (1993) *Planning and evaluating disability information services.* Policy Studies Institute

Yelding, David, Rigg, Malcolm and More O'Ferrall, Elizabeth (1993) *NDIP evaluation: interim report.* Research Institute for Consumer Affairs

7 The evaluation team

The evaluation of the National Disability Information Project is essential. People responsible for developing information and advice services need to know what works and what does not; they need to be able to understand the different models of service provision so that they can apply them to their own circumstances. The Department of Health needs to know whether NDIP achieved its objectives and whether it represented value for money. More generally, the government needs to be able to evaluate whether or not development projects like NDIP are an effective way to bring about social and organisational change.

The Department of Health decided that, in accordance with departmental policy, the evaluation team should be kept separate from the operational aspects of NDIP. The work was therefore commissioned and financed by the Research Branch of the Department and the evaluation team make their reports to this branch rather than to the policy branch that commissioned and financed NDIP.

The contract for the evaluation was placed with the Research Institute for Consumer Affairs (RICA). This is a research organisation founded by the Consumers Association. A central strand of RICA's work is concerned with disability issues. It ranges from product testing, the compilation of information guides and research on the information-provision process. Within RICA the evaluation project was led by the Research Director, supported by the Head of the Information Unit at the Consumers Association, and two staff recruited for the project.

Even though the evaluators were separate from the operational elements, it was clear from the outset that their work needed to be fitted in with the rest of NDIP. Each pilot project, for example, was encouraged to establish procedures to evaluate its work and the results of this evaluation needed to be fed into the RICA evaluation. Similarly, the project team were in a position where they were monitoring and reviewing the work of the pilot projects and trying to encapsulate the lessons learned into guidelines that could be used more widely. These processes inevitably involved a significant amount of assessment, even though evaluation was not an overt part of the process.

The RICA evaluation had three main aims:

- To evaluate the overall success of the project, its strengths and weaknesses.

- To provide information that will be of practical help to those involved in providing information for people with disabilities in the future.

- To provide information to guide government departments and other organisations which might be setting up projects which share some of the features of NDIP.

Within these aims the evaluation team set out to monitor the overall development of NDIP, and the work and involvement of the key players – the Department of Health, steering group, project team, national information providers and pilot projects. Although the process has been continuous, RICA's interim report (More O'Ferrall and others, 1993) focused on the work that NDIP had carried out with the national information providers and on the steering group. It gave an outline of work in progress and planned for the remainder of the project.

The evaluation team are also investigating some of the wider issues raised by the project, such as multi-agency working, management committees, databases and the involvement of disabled people.

Criteria and expectations

The Department of Health established a number of criteria by which NDIP should be evaluated. At the national level the criteria were concerned with the promotion of closer working relationships; the reduction of duplication and improvements in the relevance and accuracy of information. At the local level the criteria included encouraging the development of information federations; achieving greater coordination; broadening the access to information; improving the working relationships between members of federations and improving the quality, accessibility and relevance of information provided locally.

The evaluation team are also measuring NDIP against the criteria originally set by the Department of Health and discussed by the steering group. However, the brief requires RICA to make recommendations about the future structure of disability information provision. To do this they have collected the opinions of national and local organisations and individuals closely involved with disability information services, and these views will contribute to their conclusions.

Evaluation activity

The evaluation was based on information collected in a number of different ways. The evaluation team interviewed a large number of individuals involved in the Project. These interviews included people working in the national information providers, civil servants in the Department of Health, members of the Project Steering Group, workers in the pilot projects, members of management committees and people working in other organisations concerned with disability and with information and advice.

To supplement the interviews the team has drawn on internal and published documents and has spent a considerable amount of time observing the way in which processes operated. Members of the team, for example, sat in on the project team's six-monthly reviews of the pilot projects, working groups and a selection of federation and management meetings. In addition, they have carried out two surveys of the national information providers, a survey of local organisations providing disability information and a survey of organisations on the periphery of the project, such as social services departments, health authorities and community health councils.

It was not possible or appropriate to undertake a national survey of consumer opinions. The team felt that the variety of different approaches adopted by the pilot projects and the differences in the timescales made such a survey impractical. Instead, RICA has carried out research which has focused on particular aspects of consumer opinion. This has included interviewing people who have used NDIP advice services and recruiting a panel of disabled people to try out telephone services.

Finally the team has undertaken original research into the major problems and issues that have been raised by NDIP. These issues include the compilation and management of databases and directories; the concept and operation of information federations; the dissemination of information; the involvement of disabled people; the role of management committees and the overall process, structure and financing of federations.

Results

The evaluation team published an interim report covering the establishment of NDIP; the initial work with national information providers and the role of the steering group in 1993 (More O'Ferrall and others, 1993). The final results will be published in a series of reports during 1995.

References

More O'Ferrall, Elizabeth and others (1993) *Evaluation of the National Disability Information Project: Interim report and summary of work in progress*. Research Institute for Consumer Affairs

8   National information providers

It is commonly the case in libraries and information services that about 80 per cent of the enquiries are answered through reference to about 20 per cent of the information materials. This 80/20 rule also seems to apply to disability information. There is a vast amount of information available, yet a large proportion of the enquiries made by disabled people can be answered by reference to information produced by a relatively small core of national providers.

Clearly, the priority should be to try to improve the effectiveness of this core of providers.

As we noted in Chapter 6, it is possible to group national disability information providers into three categories (Hinkley and Steele, 1992):

- *National disability information providers*
  They operate at a national level providing information that is aimed at all, or a large proportion of disabled people. They cover broad, general subjects like aids and equipment or benefits.

- *Specific disability information providers*
  They also operate at a national level, providing information aimed at a more specific audience. These organisations cover subjects related to a specific disability or impairment, or a more specialised subject area, such as the use of computers for learners who have special educational needs.

- *Generalist information providers*
  These organisations provide information for general consumption, some of which will be concerned with disability issues

The national disability information providers, as we have defined them, are organisations concerned with the provision of information that is of interest to all or a large proportion of disabled people. They are organisations that have information-giving as one of their primary functions and they usually devote a substantial proportion of their resources to information activities.

Some of these organisations, like the Disabled Living Foundation or RADAR, have been in existence for many years and have become established as large and relatively well-resourced bodies providing a sophisticated information service or set of information products. Such organisations have frequently made effective use of information technology and some, notably the Disabled Living Foundation, have experimented with the delivery of information in electronic formats.

Other national information providers have been established more recently to fill perceived gaps in the overall pattern of information provision. Organisations such as the Disability Alliance and the Centre for Accessible Environments were established in the late 1970s with quite tightly defined terms of reference. Such organisations are less well resourced and, in general, employ many fewer staff than some of the longer-established bodies.

A few of the national information providers are controlled by disabled people in the formal sense that their constitution requires that disabled people form the majority on the main decision-making body. Most, however, do not have that constitutional requirement.

Most of the national information providers are registered charities with information provision as one of their charitable purposes. They are generally heavily dependent on financial support from the government. Such support is usually provided through Section 64 of the *Health Services and Public Health Act 1968*. This act gives Ministers of Health the power to make grants to voluntary bodies in England and it has been used as the main vehicle for support of national organisations concerned with disability.

Increasingly, the national information providers are having to raise a significant proportion of their income through trading activities. This usually means the sale of information products such as books and databases, or through levying charges on users of an information service. In some cases, the amount raised through such trading activities is very significant – over 30 per cent of turnover. In other cases the level of income generated through trading is low in relation to turnover.

Some national information providers, like RADAR or Age Concern, have a network of local branches. Others have membership schemes that ensure that they have regular contact with organisations and individuals operating at local level.

There are also variations in the target audience for the information provided by the different organisations. While it is true that in nearly all cases, the information is used by disabled people, carers, local information and advice services and by professionals, there is a degree of differentiation.

Some, such as the Disabled Living Foundation, clearly target their main information products at professionals, particularly occupational therapists. Others regard local information and advice services as an important segment of their market, while yet others aim to provide information direct to disabled people themselves.

It is clear from this description that there is considerable variation among the national information providers. The organisations have some common characteristics but by no means do they form a homogeneous group.

This is reflected in the level and quality of the service that they offer. Some provide sophisticated and comprehensive databases, others can provide detailed advocacy, counselling or consultancy services. In some other cases, the service offered is more basic. Much depends on the scale of resources that they have available and the priority that is given to information provision.

The national information providers are not, as we have noted, the sole providers of disability information operating at national level. It is also necessary to take account of the providers of information to specific groups or about specific conditions. There are very many information providers of this kind. The Help for Health database, for example, lists over 1,200 organisations of this kind. Nearly all self-help groups, national associations and support organisations have information provision as one of their functions. Collectively they provide an enormous amount of information, much of which is unobtainable from any other source.

These organisations are firmly in the voluntary sector and are nearly all registered charities. They vary enormously in size and sophistication from small single-person bodies to quite large organisations with a turnover measured in hundreds of thousands of pounds and a network of local groups.

Like the national information providers, these organisations are, in many cases, reliant on financial support from central government. They also depend increasingly on income generated through trading activities and fund raising and many raise money by selling information products or by charging for information services.

Finally, it is necessary to acknowledge the role played by national organisations that provide information relevant to disabled people even though only a small part of it is targeted specifically at them – the generalist information providers. Organisations like the Child Poverty Action Group, the National Association of Citizens Advice Bureaux or Shelter, for example, provide information services and products for disabled people, as well as more general information to meet needs which may be experienced by anyone at some time.

Much could be gained from greater integration of the diverse sources of information for disabled people. Such integration needs to operate at two different levels. Nationally there would be value in closer working between the information providers. Currently there are relatively few opportunities for information providers to exchange experience and to learn from each other. There may also be value in adopting common approaches to certain problems – the pre-classification of information is a case in point.

It is, however, at the interaction between the national and local levels that the need for better integration is greatest. Currently there is relatively little contact between disability information providers operating nationally and the local sources of information and advice. There are, of course, exceptions: the Disabled Living Foundation has considerable experience of working with local occupational therapists; the Disability Alliance is well-regarded by local disability information and advice services. In general, however, there is a depressingly low level of awareness on both sides. The national providers do not have good links with the local services that could transmit their information to the people who need it. Equally, most local information and advice services use only a fraction of the information that is available from national providers (Barnes, 1994).

It seems evident that the overall provision of information for disabled people would be improved if the activities at national level were integrated more closely with those at a local level. In particular, there is a need for better communication between national and local providers. Such communication would provide a better means of identifying gaps and areas of need, ensuring that the information made available nationally fully meets the needs of the ultimate users. It would also provide a useful quality control mechanism as local information and advice workers would, in many cases, be in a better position to assess the strengths and weaknesses of information products and services than would the information users who would have little comparative experience on which to base their judgements.

Greater integration almost certainly means moving towards a system where there is more specialisation. The national organisations are in the best position to specialise in the collection and processing of information, making it available as information products or services that can be used by the local information and advice services. Equally the local information and advice services, whether provided by specialist agencies, groups of disabled people or by professionals, are best placed to provide the direct services to the disabled people themselves and to build the kind of relationship between provider and user that is most likely to ensure that disabled people's long-term information needs are met effectively. This is not to say that there is no direct information provision role for the national providers. Such direct contact with information users can play an important part in keeping the national information workers in touch with the issues. It does, however, suggest that the national and local organisations offer complementary services. And that they should build on each other's strengths.

Funding national disability information provision

The funding system for national disability information services is dominated by Section 64 of the *Health Services and Public Health Act 1968*. This is the Department of Health's main channel of grant aid to the voluntary sector. Through it grants totalling £19.25 million will be made to voluntary organisations working in the field of health and personal social services during 1994-95. About 300 voluntary organisations will be supported in this way.

The grants are made available to organisations that undertake activities that further the Department's policy objectives. Increasingly this is being interpreted as testing an innovatory idea or helping to develop a particular pattern of service.

There are four types of grant: core grants to assist with the central administrative costs of a national organisation; national project grants to support innovatory or development projects that are in line with Departmental policy objectives; local project grants where a project is clearly innovatory, of national significance and in line with Departmental objectives, and capital grants which are relatively rare.

It appears that there has been a fairly major policy shift within the Department of Health. Emphasis has moved away from core grants and turned towards project grants. The reasons for this are clear. Since the introduction of the Act, a number of organisations have come to rely on Section 64 as their main source of funds. The size of the core grant has grown steadily as inflation and the gradual increase in activities and responsibilities have had their effect. The result is a situation where the majority of Section 64 funds are effectively committed to funding the core activities of well-established organisations.

This would perhaps not be a problem in a period when the economy was expanding steadily and when there was relatively little downward pressure on public expenditure. But government policy on public expenditure and the economic conditions of the last few years have put the overall budget under increasing pressure. One effect of this has been that newer organisations – those that have come into being in the last decade – have found it increasingly difficult to get their feet under the table.

Even allowing for growth above the rate of inflation – the Section 64 budget increased by four per cent in 1994-95 – the Department has also found that the discretionary element – the amount uncommitted each year after continuing commitments are taken into account – has been squeezed and this has constrained its ability to use the money to stimulate innovation.

So, recipients of Section 64 core funds have effectively been served notice. Essentially, they can look forward to one more renewal for no more than five years. And they can expect to see the value of the grant tapering off towards the end of that period. Under such circumstances they face two main choices. They can try to obtain funding from other sources. Or they can try to redefine their core activities as a series of projects, each of which might be eligible for project grants.

This is the position facing the national providers of disability information. The well-established organisations are finding their core budgets under severe threat and are having to make substantial savings. While the newer, less well-established organisations are facing future reductions in core support that was anyway felt to be inadequate.

The message for the future is that Section 64 may become a powerful means of stimulating innovation and for pump-priming new services, but it is unlikely to cover the day-to-day expenses of organisations.

There is, however, a strong case to be made for continuing central government support. Economies of scale and the savings that can be made by avoiding duplication point to the need for effective services at national level. It would not, for example, make sense for every local disability information and advice service to attempt to collect information about the full range of aids and equipment that is available. Equally, it would be unrealistic to expect local services to have access to the kind of specialist advice that is a characteristic of a service like the Centre for Accessible Environments. Similarly, a local service could never expect to build up the depth of expertise that is to be found in an organisation like the Disability Alliance.

What is needed is a system that builds on national and local strengths. One in which national organisations can use their economies of scale and specialist expertise to produce information products and services that can be used to support the direct information and advice services that are provided locally.

References

Barnes, Colin (1994) *From national to local: an evaluation of the effectiveness of national disablement information providers' services to local disablement information providers.* British Council of Organisations of Disabled People

Hinkley, Philipa and Steele, Jane (1992) *National disability information provision: sources and issues.* Policy Studies Institute

9   Local disability information and advice services

In England there are nearly 600 local services providing information and advice for disabled people (Nadash, 1993). The local information and advice services, like their national counterparts, vary widely. Some, like the members of the DIAL UK network, have a policy of being controlled and staffed by disabled people or people with personal experience of disability. Their primary function is the provision of information and advice. In other cases, groups provide an information service but do so only as one of a range of different functions.

In some parts of the country, disability information and advice services operate as part of a federation. The federations provide a means of coordinating a range of local information provision. They also provide a way of sharing information, experience and the costs of certain activities that are best carried out jointly.

Important contributors of information at local level are the local groups or branches of national organisations. In many cases these, for obvious reasons, have a specific focus, but they frequently extend their information services beyond their immediate target audience.

These specialist disability information and advice services are complemented by a range of information and advice services. Britain is fortunate in having what is probably the world's most sophisticated network of information and advice services. There are, for example, 712 citizens advice bureaux and over 1,000 independent information and advice services offering generalist advice. These are complemented both by specialist services provided by law centres, housing aid services, consumer advice agencies and others and by services for specific sectors of the community such as black and ethnic minorities.

In addition, information and advice is provided by professionals concerned with the well-being of disabled people. These range from occupational therapists to specialist staff in the Benefits Agency. Some are employed in the health service, others are employed by local authorities, usually in social services. Others, such as the Benefits Agency staff, may be employed by a national organisation but they operate at a local level, often working closely with disability information and advice services.

Disability information federations

The existence of NDIP has undoubtedly stimulated the development of federations. Not only were many formed to bid for NDIP funds but the project itself has drawn attention to the concept. As we have seen, federations were advocated but not defined in the Coopers and Lybrand report (1988). The work carried out by PE International took things a step further and set out three possible models of a federation: centralised, radial and cascade.

- The *centralised* model was based on a single enquiry point which would hold and maintain a database and use it to respond to questions. The federation members would act as a steering group ensuring that the information provided was appropriate to local needs.

- The *radial* model would have a central enquiry point linked to satellite enquiry points, each satellite being a member of the federation. The federation members collectively would act as the steering group for the federation.

- The *cascade* model would have satellites that were not single organisations but sub- or mini-federations. This model was thought to be appropriate for large counties.

The federations within NDIP did not conform to these models. They were all different: they had different structures, different objectives, different philosophies and different ways of working.

A similar degree of variety was apparent in the federations that had been unsuccessful in their bids to NDIP. In 1992, to explore this diversity further, we conducted a survey of disability information federations. We approached all the organisations that had submitted applications to become pilot projects and we approached other federations that were known to exist. We found that of the 95 projects we approached only 29 were still in operation (Simpkins and Nadash, 1993).

We also found that they too did not conform to the models identified by PE International. This may well have been a direct result of the fact that they had very little funding and could, therefore, do little more than exchange information between members.

The models were based mainly on the organisational structures. They failed to allow for variations in the nature of the work undertaken. In particular, only a minority of the federations studied provided a direct service to the public from the central or core unit of the federation. It was more common for the central unit of a federation to provide support services to federation members or to undertake development and coordination work. Yet direct service provision is implicit in all three of the PE International models.

There was so much variation that it is difficult to develop models that more accurately correspond to the federations that were operating in 1992. It was, however, possible to identify two broad approaches.

The most common approach consisted of a small central unit that provided resources – usually a local database and some training – to a number of local information and advice services. The central unit provided a focus for service development and planning. In some cases the central unit also provided a public enquiry service. In most cases the local services acted as federation members and collectively controlled the central unit. Federations that conformed to this broad model operated in: Berkshire, Buckinghamshire, Devon, Gateshead, Gloucestershire, Hertfordshire, Kent, Lambeth, Lancashire, Norfolk, Northamptonshire, Oxfordshire, Somerset and Surrey.

The second approach was similar to the centralised model described by PE International. Here a number of interested organisations had joined together to contribute to a single, centralised information and advice service. This approach was common in urban areas. Services of this kind were found in Carlisle, Keighley, Leeds and the Wirral.

In other cases information and advice services were provided by groups like coalitions of disabled people that had extensive links with other organisations. The Greater London Association of Disabled People and the Huntingdonshire Coalition of Disabled People were examples of this types of service. It is, however, stretching the definition of information federations a little far to include such groups.

It is interesting to note that in the Coopers and Lybrand report, part of the rationale for federations was the fact that they provided an opportunity to bring the statutory and voluntary sectors together. Indeed the requirement to have both statutory and voluntary sector participation was one of criteria for application to NDIP. Yet 11 of the non-pilot federations were restricted to organisations from the voluntary sector.

Other local services
Federations are not the dominant form of local information and advice provision for disabled people. Much more common are the independent information and advice centres and the advice services provided by local groups of national organisations.

In 1992-93 we tried to identify as many local services as possible. In part we wanted to explore the nature of existing services and to identify any gaps in provision. We also hoped that, by publishing the results in the form of a directory we would promote contact between groups. We actually identified over 600 local information and advice services for disabled people (Nadash, 1993).

Within any locality, disabled people can approach a range of organisations for information and advice. We were particularly interested in the organisations that specialised in information and advice work and that set out to meet the specific needs of disabled people. This meant excluding a large number of other providers.

First we excluded the groups that were only able to provide information on a narrow range of disability issues, perhaps because they were concerned with a particular condition or impairment. We did, however, include information services offered by local groups of Age Concern, Mencap and MIND on the grounds that they each covered significant proportions of the disabled population.

We excluded groups that had a very broad information and advice remit which covered much more than disability issues. Thus citizens advice bureaux and other generalist advice services were excluded. We also excluded specialist information and advice services that were aimed at the general public as distinct from disabled people. On these grounds we excluded housing aid services, health information services, educational advisory services and consumer advice centres.

We also excluded groups that, as part of their other activities, would provide information if someone asked for it but for which information and advice was not one of their main functions. Finally, we excluded professionals and social services departments.

Through these exclusions we were able to focus on the 600 or more local groups that devoted resources to the provision of an advertised information and advice service for disabled people.

The pattern of provision was fairly even over the country. Local services were available in most major towns and in a surprising number of predominantly rural areas.

Many services were offered by groups of disabled people and they were often associated with campaigning work. Other services were provided by local groups of Age Concern, Mencap and MIND.

Networks

In addition to the information and advice services provided by local groups of Age Concern, Mencap and MIND, many of the groups belonged to one of the national networks of advice services.

Of these, the most prominent is DIAL UK. This was established in 1977 to bring together the growing number of DIAL (Disability Information and Advice Line) services. Membership of the network grew rapidly in the early 1980s and by 1983 DIAL UK represented 54 local groups. By 1990 the number had risen to 78 and in 1994 100 local groups were in membership. Together they dealt with over 245,000 enquiries in 1994.

DIAL UK provides its members with a number of services including training and a monthly information service. One of the main functions of DIAL UK is to represent the views of its members at a national level. To assist this it is a member of the Advice Services Alliance, the umbrella organisation that represents the main networks of advice services.

Eighty local groups belong to the Federation of Information and Advice Centres (FIAC). This was established at the same time as DIAL UK but is open to all forms of independent advice service. It currently has over 850 services in membership. FIAC provides its members with training and specialist services like access to pension and insurance schemes. It also provides local advice services with a voice at national level and is a member of the Advice Services Alliance.

A number of disability advice services are provided by citizens advice bureaux which are, of course members of their national association – NACAB. As members they receive the monthly information service and have access to the training and other centrally provided services. One of NACAB's stated aims is to feed back to policy-makers information about the consequences of their policies and, along with DIAL UK and FIAC it has, for example, provided the Department of Social Security with a great deal of information about the practical problems that were associated with the introduction of the revised disability benefits in 1992.

The National Association of Disability Information and Advice Federations (NADIAF) was formed to represent and promote disability information federations. It was originally called CHOICE. It is a loose association and, unlike DIAL UK, FIAC and NACAB, does not have membership criteria: membership is open to any individual or group that supports the concept of information federations.

The other network of local advice services is the Disabled Living Centres Council. This represents local disabled living centres.

It is not yet possible to say that the local services operate as an overall information system. There is too much fragmentation and, while many, if not most, of the services belong to one or other of the national networks, there are still a significant number that are operating in isolation. There are, however, signs that the situation is changing. The Alliance of Disability Information Providers that has been formed by the main networks to carry forward the work that was started by NDIP is, perhaps, the first step towards a unified approach to the development of an active network of local disability information and advice services.

References

Coopers and Lybrand (1988) *Information needs of disabled people, their carers and service providers*. Department of Health and Social Security

Nadash, Pamela (1993) *Directory of local disability information providers*. Policy Studies Institute

Simpkins, Rebecca and Nadash, Pamela (1993) *Disability information federations: features and issues*. Policy Studies Institute

Part III

The achievements

A great deal has happened in three years. The NDIP pilot projects have developed their services. National information providers have considered a range of issues that could lead to improvements in their information products and services. New information systems have become available.

It seems certain too, that the number of local advice services for disabled people has increased and that the quality of provision has improved. The networks that support the local services are better established and are working together more constructively than they were three years ago.

How much of this is due to the National Disability Information Project? Has NDIP brought about change? Or has the project itself simply been a reflection of a more far-reaching process of development? Has the impetus of NDIP been confined to the pilot projects? Or have there been wider repercussions affecting the general provision of information and advice for disabled people?

Are disabled people better informed and advised now than they were three years ago?

One way to answer these questions is to return to the aims and objectives that were established at the outset and to assess the changes that have taken place. In this way it is possible to identify the achievements of NDIP and to arrive at a judgement of their likely long-term impact.

Part III – Contents

10 Aims and objectives

To begin, we have to return to the aims and objectives: the statement of what we set out to achieve.

In any large project it is important that everyone involved has a clear understanding of the aims and objectives. Ideally, they should not just understand but should actively endorse them. In a wide-ranging project like NDIP, it was also important to give each of the different interest groups an opportunity to contribute to the formulation of the aims and objectives.

NDIP began with a fairly broad statement of purpose from the Department. At the launch conference it became possible to refine this a little by identifying the priorities for development. Following the conference the project team drafted a set of aims and objectives for consideration by the project steering group. The draft was also made available to the pilot projects. After some discussion, both groups endorsed the draft and it was made available through the *NDIP Newsletter* for wider consideration.

It is interesting to note that at none of these stages were any significant modifications made to the draft aims and objectives. This possibly reflects a strong consensus about the issues, and their relative priorities and a general agreement about what it was that NDIP should be trying to achieve.

Aims
The broad purpose of NDIP was to improve the provision of information for disabled people, their carers and professional advisers. This was to be achieved through the twin aims which were specified at the outset by the Department of Health. These were:

- *Nationally,* to improve the effectiveness of the national information providers and to promote greater coordination.

- *Locally,* to encourage the development of effective local information services.

Objectives

It was necessary to translate these aims into operational terms. To do this, the project team specified a number of long-term objectives:

- To ensure that all services fully meet the needs of their users.

- To ensure that there is an adequate supply of appropriate information.

- To ensure that there is an even pattern of provision throughout the country.

- To ensure that there is an adequate and stable source of funding for the information services.

- To ensure that services are provided by well-trained and, where appropriate, well-paid staff.

- To ensure that information service providers have access to cheap, reliable and effective information systems.

- To ensure that the development of information services for disabled people does not take place in isolation.

- To ensure that there is an infrastructure which will encourage and support further development.

It is important to stress that these were *long-term* objectives. It would have been unrealistic to expect to achieve all this within the space of three years. The intention was to give a clear indication of the goals that we were pursuing and the directions in which we were going.

The objectives also served as a statement of the criteria that we felt an effective disability information and advice service should conform to. In this context, it is necessary to elaborate each objective a little to set out the rationale that lies behind them.

Meeting the needs of users

There is clearly little point in developing information services which do not meet the needs of the users they set out to serve. One of the tasks of the project was to consider how users' needs are best satisfied and how services can be constituted so that users are empowered by the information they receive.

Providers must address the need to make sure that users are actively encouraged to play a major role in the design, development and the delivery of the services. Some providers hold strongly to the view that the services should be provided, managed or controlled by people with disabilities or at least by people with first hand experience of disability. In other cases service providers believe that users can be involved through a process of consultation.

Adequate and appropriate information

At all levels there must be adequate access to appropriate information. The general objective should be to ensure that the right information is available in the right format for the right person in the right place at the right time. Some might add, 'at the right price'.

To achieve this is no easy task. To do so, it would be necessary to ensure that information providers, whether operating at national or local level, meet acceptable standards of quality and accessibility. In particular it is essential to ensure that information which is disseminated is fully accessible by all who need it. This means that a variety of formats need to be considered, including large print, Braille, and audio tape.

It also means that the information itself needs to be designed and communicated so that it is comprehensible by, and relevant to, the particular circumstances of the widest possible range of people. In this context it is important to acknowledge the role of advisers who can tailor the information and advice to suit different individuals.

Further, it is important to ensure that national information is made available in accessible formats at affordable prices.

An even pattern of provision

At the beginning of NDIP it was thought that the local provision of disability information was patchy and uneven. Indeed, the award of funding to 12 pilot projects might be seen as exacerbating that unevenness. We aimed to encourage provision in areas where nothing existed. In other areas, through the project, we attempted to encourage cooperation and coordination among providers.

It is, however, important to acknowledge the need for local services to reflect local circumstances and needs. We did not, therefore, feel that it was either possible or desirable to produce universally applicable blueprints, or standard models of provision.

Adequate and stable funding

The development of advice and information services over the last twenty years has been constrained and distorted by funding difficulties. In particular, the dependence on annually renewed grants has meant that service providers have, of necessity, adopted a short-term approach to planning.

A variety of funding possibilities and options are now available, notably those which result from the emerging contract culture in health and social service authorities. Local disability information and advice services should be encouraged to explore and to exploit these arrangements.

The aim is to ensure that local and national providers have access to adequate and stable sources of funding which enable services to be developed in a planned and organised manner.

Well-trained and well-paid staff

Providing information that is tailored to meet a person's particular needs is a complex task that calls for particular skills and abilities. High quality services will need to be delivered by high quality staff. This means that there is a significant need for training. This need will continue indefinitely and so it was important to establish, or to encourage the development of, permanent training facilities.

It also raised questions about the extent to which services depend on volunteer staff. The use of volunteers is undoubtedly an important element in the development of an emergent public service. We have to accept, however, that the effectiveness of volunteers is increased greatly when they are able to work within a framework coordinated by full-time paid staff.

Cheap, reliable and effective information systems

There is clearly great scope for using information and communications technology to deliver information for disabled people. To realise this potential, information providers, whether operating at local or national level, need access to cheap, reliable and effective information systems.

It was important to achieve a balance between what is technically possible and what is practically feasible. Within NDIP, some pilot projects made significant use of technology and it was important to transfer the lessons learned so that other services could benefit.

Development in isolation

Information and advice services for disabled people should not develop in isolation. At the beginning of NDIP there were already over 2,000 information and advice services in the voluntary sector. These services and the networks that support them contained a substantial amount of experience and expertise which could make a contribution to the successful development of information and advice services for disabled people. It was important to establish and maintain contact with the networks at both national and local levels.

Local services also need to acknowledge the fact that disabled people will continue to use services like the citizens advice bureaux to satisfy many of their needs. It was important to work with these services to ensure that they can accommodate, in every sense of the word, the needs of disabled people.

A continuing infrastructure

The development of information services for disabled people will not end with the completion of NDIP. It was therefore essential to develop and strengthen the infrastructure which will be needed to maintain the momentum of change.

The potential existed for NDIP to work with bodies like DIAL UK, FIAC, NADIAF and the National Information Forum to develop services and facilities which will have a life beyond that of the Project.

In these and in other ways NDIP sought to develop and promote the provision of information services for disabled people and their carers.

11   Meeting the needs of users

There is clearly little point in establishing services that do not meet the needs of their users. In a commercial environment, such services would go out of business. In a non-commercial environment, however, things are less certain. In some circumstances, it is possible for public services to carry on for a long time without actually meeting real needs.

To assess the extent to which services do meet the needs of their users it is necessary first to decide who those users are and then to consider the type of services that are required to meet their needs.

The users of disability information and advice services
Disability information and advice services are used by three broad groups of people: disabled people themselves, carers and personal assistants of disabled people, and professionals. Each group has different characteristics that call for a different type of service.

Disabled people
The OPCS survey of disabled people in 1985 estimated that there were 6.2 million disabled adults in Great Britain (Office of Population Censuses and Surveys, 1988 and 1989). The same survey estimated there were 360,000 disabled children. A more recent report, *The economic problems of disabled people*, estimated that by 1993 there were 6.9 million disabled adults (Berthoud, Lakey and McKay, 1993).

Disabled people and their families have higher living costs than other families. What is more, the combination of reduced income and higher costs means that many disabled people are likely to be worse off financially than other members of the population and increasingly reliant on social security benefits.

The OPCS survey suggested that less than a third of disabled people of working age were employed – approximately 700,000. The PSI report found that disabled people have poor chances of gaining employment and if they do, their earnings are below the average earnings of non-disabled people.

Of disabled people and their families 2.6 million live in poverty with 60 per cent of disabled people claiming safety-net benefits and 47 per cent reported as not having sufficient income to meet their minimum living costs. The income of families with disabled children was lower than that of other families and a third of families with disabled children were receiving income maintenance benefits.

Disabled people have the same range of information needs that are experienced by everyone else in society. They need information to be able to participate fully in society, to be aware of all their rights and entitlements and to ensure they can take responsibility for their own well-being. In addition, however, they have specific information needs that arise as a result of their position as disabled people. In particular, they may need information about social security, services and opportunities in areas such as housing, transport and employment. In some circumstances, restricted mobility or sensory impairment may prevent disabled people from using the general information and advice services that are available and, as a result, they require special service provision even though the information sought may be no different from that sought by non-disabled people.

Carers and personal assistants

The Carers National Association estimates that there are 6.8 million carers in the UK. The Family Expenditure Survey in 1988 showed that the household income of carers in their study were on average lower than those of the general population. A Department of Social Security study in 1990 found that carers in families with disabled children had net weekly incomes that were between £58 and £92 lower than those of comparable households in the general population.

Carers are also not a single homogeneous group; their information needs will be just as complex and varied as those of disabled people. They may even be made more complex by the fact they are not only seeking information for themselves as carers, but often seeking information on behalf of the disabled person.

Carers may have difficulty in accessing information. They may be unaware of what information is available and where it can be obtained. The situation can be compounded by the fact that many carers do not identify themselves as such. Although they may not have mobility problems or sensory impairments which restrict access to information, their role as carer will limit the time and resources they have available to seek help.

Personal assistants are in a slightly different category from most carers. They will be, in effect, employees of the disabled person and as a consequence will be likely to have a very different relationship with the disabled person than a carer would have. They are more likely to seek information on the instructions of the disabled person, acting on their behalf and, perhaps, overcoming some of the problems of access that might otherwise prevent the disabled person from using a service.

Professionals

A range of professionals need disability information. They need it to function in their jobs. They also need to be sufficiently well-informed to be able to pass information on to, and to advise, disabled people.

Occupational therapists are major users of disability information. In 1993 there were 13,810 registered with their professional association. Of this total, 8,750 were known to be employed by the NHS and by local authorities in England.

In addition to the occupational therapists, there are 150 local authorities in the UK providing social services and other departments or units that are concerned with disability issues. Their information needs are considerable and are growing. The changes that have been brought about through the move towards care in the community have heightened the need for a large number of local authority staff to be well informed about the issues that have most impact on disabled people.

Increasing financial restrictions on health service and local authority funding will, no doubt, result in restricted budgets for purchasing information. The Disabled Living Foundation found that 'financial constraints' was one of the major reasons given when cancelling subscriptions to their service.

In addition to the network of advice centres that we described in chapter one, the National Welfare Rights Officers Group identifies approximately 70 welfare rights units operating in the various local authorities in the UK. In some authorities they are associated with consumer and housing advice units.

General practitioners are often cited as potential sources of information and advice for disabled people. GPs may be in a good position to provide information on medical matters but they are, however, unwilling to undertake a wider information role, recognising that they are not sufficiently well-informed themselves (Perkins, Roberts and Moore, 1992).

Conclusion

There are clear differences between these groups of users. Disabled people, their carers and assistants will have intermittent needs for information. That is to say, they will need to have information or advice to solve a problem but once that problem is solved the need for information passes. In contrast a professional will need to have constant access to information in order to function effectively.

Professionals will expect to receive information that takes account of their level of expertise and prior knowledge. They will be (reasonably) happy dealing with jargon and they can be expected to become familiar with information products and services that incorporate relatively complex search strategies. They will expect to supplement the basic information with their own professional knowledge and expertise.

Disabled people, their carers and assistants, on the other hand will probably not be so receptive to jargon. In certain areas closely related to their impairment or disability they are likely to be more familiar with technicalities and jargon as the professionals but once outside those areas their level of prior knowledge will tail off. Their intermittent use of information sources means that they will not be in a position where they can become familiar with complex search processes.

Because of these factors, disabled people, their carers and assistants, like everyone else, are likely to have a need for advice and assistance when using information. They will need specialist help to tailor information to their particular circumstances, interpreting entitlements and assessing eligibility for services. They are also likely to need advice on the strategy and tactics to adopt when pursuing a course of action and, indeed, may need encouragement and assistance to follow the action through. We will discuss below who is best placed to provide that advice.

In short, professionals need information and can handle information that is presented in relatively sophisticated packages. The other users need information and advice. For them information comes best when wrapped in a knowledgeable person.

Special provision

We have to consider whether or not disabled people need special provision. If they do, why do they need it?

Disabled people need specialist information and advice provision for three principal reasons: other public information and advice services are not accessible; disabled people have particular subject needs that would not be addressed by generalist services and disabled people need the be able to draw on the personal experience of other disabled people.

Disabled people find that most public information and advice services are inaccessible. This is more than simply a question of being able to get a wheelchair through the door of a Benefits Agency local office or the CAB. It is a much wider issue about the accessibility of information. Generally speaking, we are not good at making information available in formats that are accessible by minority groups within the population. Whether it is the production of leaflets in the languages of minority ethnic communities, or the availability of British Sign Language interpreters in hospitals, the record in Britain is generally poor. In most cases, where provision is made, it is done as an exception – a facility that can be made available on demand.

The reasons for this are not hard to find. Mostly it comes down to a question of cost. It is expensive to make information available in multiple formats. To make all information available in large print, in Braille, on audio tape, on computer disc, in BSL and in formats appropriate for people with learning difficulties would add significantly to the costs of the information providers.

There is also a lack of awareness among information providers of the need to make information available in these formats. In this context it is interesting to note that information provision in minority ethnic languages increased significantly following the passage of the *Race Relations Act 1976*. The legislation, while not compelling organisations to publish in minority languages, almost certainly served to raise awareness of the need to do so.

Until all information is available in accessible formats, it will be necessary to have some forms of special provision to provide disabled people with the access they need.

Even if the general public information and advice services were accessible, there would still be a need for special services to meet the need for information on the subjects that are particular to disability and impairment. These needs are extensive, ranging from expertise in disability benefits, through aids and equipment to information about specific conditions or impairments.

Finally, disabled people need to be able to benefit from the experience of other disabled people. In her address to the 1993 NDIP conference, Frances Hasler, the Director of the Greater London Association of Disabled People, argued forcefully that the information that disabled people need most 'is that which comes from the disabled experience' and, consequently disabled people need to inform each other. She goes on to say:

> I am suggesting that most of what is thought of as disability information
> is what could be characterised as consumer information or impairment
> information. What disabled people need to know is far more profound

than benefits, holidays, incontinence, charities, although it may include all these things. It is quite literally how to live, how to participate as equal citizens. The only way to find that out is through a centre for independent living or at least through an organisation which has the ethos of one (Hasler, 1993).

On the basis of this analysis, it appears that there will be a continuing need for some form of information and advice provision that is aimed specifically at meeting the needs of disabled people.

The nature of the service

There is a considerable body of research and experience that can be drawn upon to provide an indication of what type of service users need. The clear indication is that what people need is an easily accessible source of informed advice that can provide information tailored to suit the individual's particular circumstances.

A recent publication from PSI provides a useful starting point for a consideration of the needs for, and the use of information and advice services. The review covered over 150 separate research studies and provides the best available overall picture of information and advice needs (Bryson and Kempson, 1994). The review was particularly concerned with information and advice about benefits but many of the findings are generally applicable – enquiries about benefits anyway form the largest proportion of enquiries in most disability information and advice services.

The conclusion to be drawn from the research is that information, in the form of posters, leaflets, or broadcast advertising, was effective in raising awareness of benefits but that this awareness alone was not sufficient to cause people to make a claim. A range of attitudinal barriers inhibited claiming and people needed help to overcome these barriers. The review cites the conclusions of a study carried out by Peter Craig of the DSS who argued that we need to

...focus on ways of sharpening perceptions of eligibility rather than just increasing general awareness of the existence of benefits. Other methods of improving understanding, such as the provision of informed advice or the encouragement to claim, should also be considered as a way of supplementing publicity (Craig, 1991).

The key here is 'informed advice'. Many studies have shown that, when faced with a problem, people turned first to another person (Cragg Ross and Dawson, 1990; Hedges and Ritchie, 1988; Tester and Meredith, 1987). In many cases, however, they turned to friends, relations and neighbours who were little wiser than they. People were frequently found to be dissatisfied with the information they received from these sources.

People also turned to the professionals with whom they came into contact. But the professionals themselves felt that they were not well enough informed to be able to meet people's information needs other than in the narrow context of their professional specialism (Perkins, Roberts and Moore, 1992).

There was a general need for an active advice service that was independent of the service providers and that could tailor information to meet the needs of the client, acting on their behalf where necessary (BJM Research Partners, 1991; Kempson, 1987).

People needed different things from information and advice services. In the context of welfare benefits people's needs changed when they started to claim the benefit. Before making a claim they needed help to interpret the benefit regulations and to assess whether or not they were entitled to that particular benefit. They also needed to calculate whether they would actually be better off claiming that benefit, or whether, by claiming they would lose entitlement to other benefits (this 'better-off' calculation, as it is known, is complex and a number of computer-based systems have been developed to enable advice workers to make the calculation). Once they had made the claim and had entered the system they needed help to negotiate with the Benefits Agency (Hedges and Ritchie, 1988).

These different information and advice needs are met in different ways by different agencies. Service providers have a major role to play in providing the information and guidance up to the point where people make a claim. Once in the system, however, the emphasis shifts to independent advice agencies.

In the context of the benefits system, for example, the Benefits Agency has accepted that it should take on the role of providing information and advice to raise awareness of benefits and to help people make a claim. To this end they have done much to improve their information provision in recent years. Once a claim has been made, however, they recognise that independent advice services have a role in supporting in the claimant in their dealings with the Benefits Agency.

A similar situation prevails in the context of the tax system. The Inland Revenue will provide a considerable amount of help to an individual wishing to enter the system as a self-employed person. Once in the system, however, the Revenue advises the individual to seek the assistance of an independent adviser or accountant. The Revenue, indeed, recognises the legitimacy of these advisers by sending all the correspondence to the adviser rather than to the individual.

There are, therefore, two related functions. First there is the provision of information to publicise and to raise awareness of goods, services or facilities. The responsibility for providing that information is usually readily accepted by the providers of the goods and services. They are also usually very keen to work with local agencies to disseminate the information.

The second function is more concerned with advising than with information dissemination. People need advisers to help them interpret information and to apply it to their own circumstances. They need help and encouragement to act on that information. And they need expert support and assistance when dealing with complex systems and bureaucracies. This advice function is usually provided by specialist agencies that are independent of the providers of the goods and services. These advisers or advice agencies may themselves need information to enable them to perform their function effectively. In the disability field, many of the national information providers exist to supply this type of information.

These ideas are not new. It is worth quoting at length from the recommendations of the National Consumer Council made nearly 20 years ago:

> All advice centres should be more aware that people have varying capacities to help themselves and that many people need more than just information or even advice if they are to get their problems solved. Therefore, we believe that advice centres should be more prepared to give practical help to those without the capacity or experience to act on the information alone. Less articulate people cannot be left to their own devices armed with nothing but a leaflet. They need the guidance and sympathy of an adviser and a helping hand through out the various stages of getting their problems solved. This is not to minimise the value of self help. There is no point in advice workers doing what people can perfectly well do for themselves. But for the diffident, the inarticulate, the apprehensive and unsure, the prospect of confronting a shop manager or an official, let alone appearing in court or before a tribunal, is a daunting one. Too often they will not do any of these things, however crucial such action may be, unless they can rely on practical support from someone whose knowledge and experience they can trust (National Consumer Council, 1977).

The subjects to be covered

The Coopers and Lybrand report suggested that the range of information that disabled people needed included the following: knowledge of their impairment and its prognosis; financial entitlements to benefits; employment; aids, adaptations and other equipment; housing and accommodation; education, training and rehabilitation; mobility; leisure and holidays; other health and social services (Coopers and Lybrand, 1988).

This list is fairly all-encompassing, even though it concentrates on what Frances Hasler described as impairment and consumer information and omits the information about living as a disabled person.

Experience from disability information and advice services indicates that the largest number of enquiries are concerned with information about money: about incomes, benefits and debts. This is not surprising for two reasons. First, income-related enquiries are the most common in generalist services: for example,they represented almost half the enquiries received by CABx in 1992-93 (National Association of Citizens Advice Bureaux, 1993). Secondly, disabled people, as we have seen, have lower than average incomes and are disproportionately dependent on benefits.

Income and money-related enquiries call for a relatively high level of skill in the adviser. The systems are complex and subject to interpretation. The problems are, in many cases, very pressing and success or failure can make a big impact on an individual's quality of life. Also the work often involves a considerable degree of negotiation by the adviser – negotiating with officers of the Benefits Agency, with representatives of creditors and often with court officials.

Housing and employment are two other major areas where advice is sought by disabled people. Again, the reasons are unsurprising. Disabled people, as a group, experience higher levels of unemployment and greater difficulties in securing employment (Martin, White and Meltzer, 1989; Prescott-Clarke, 1990). Housing is also critical for many disabled people. Their low incomes and dependence on benefits significantly reduces the degree of housing choice open to them. For some the situation is further complicated by their need for accommodation that is adapted to meet their circumstances.

Education and training is another significant area. In some cases there is a need for special education provision, in others the need might be to extricate an individual from special provision and to get them integrated into a mainstream educational service. Training needs are often linked to employment problems.

There is a need for information and advice about social services. This need has grown considerably with the move towards care in the community. The underlying philosophy of care in the community is choice. This has emphasised the need for information and advice to enable individuals to make informed choices. Here people need information about the resources and the facilities that are available; about the local authority's community care plans and about the assessments and care packages that are developed to meet individual needs (Steele and others, 1993).

Social services departments have a number of legal obligations to provide information and a number of them are sub-contracting parts of this work to the voluntary sector in recognition of the desirability of ensuring a degree of independence in the provision of the information service. The NDIP pilot project based in Gateshead has been awarded a contract from the local authority to provide just this kind of community care information service.

There is a continuing need for information about aids and equipment. A number of agencies exist to meet this need, including disabled living centres and a range of services associated with social services departments. Occupational therapists clearly play a significant part in the provision of this information.

Information about aids and equipment lends itself to presentation in the form of manuals and databases. It is concrete information about definable, and relatively easily describable, objects. It is accepted even here, however, that there is a significant need for interpretation and adaptation of the basic information to the needs of the user. Similarly, information on leisure and holidays lends itself to presentation in directories and databases.

Related to aids and equipment is information about mobility. This is, however, a broad topic that can encompass information about mobility aids, through to rights of access to public transport.

Finally, on the Coopers and Lybrand list, there is information about impairments and conditions. This type of information is often associated with health-related information and advice services and these have developed considerably since the publication of the *Patients charter*. Not surprisingly, information from such sources is often strongly influenced by its origins in the health service. Increasingly, however, these consumer health information services are emphasising the value of self-help groups. The best known consumer health service – Help for Health – has always had this provision of information about self-help groups as one of its priorities.

One subject area is missing from the Coopers and Lybrand list. It is the cluster of topics associated with independent living: information about 'a way of gaining control over basic daily activities... the means to survive' (Hasler, 1993). Here information and advice may encompass many of the subject areas described above but what is critical is the way in which the enquiries are dealt with. Here information and advice provision should be part of a process of enabling individuals to live as equals in society. (It should be noted that many advice services for non-disabled people would claim that an important part of their work was concerned with empowerment and the erosion of inequalities in society).

Information and advice services for disabled people are therefore called upon to deal with a wide range of issues and topics.

Accountability and control

It is not easy to determine in advance what users need. Users may be able to say what they *want,* but that is a rather different thing. Once services become established, however, the situation becomes easier. Put simply, if a service is not meeting people's needs, they usually stop using it: few people return to a service that has failed to deliver what they need. In contrast, a service that really does meet its users's needs usually experiences a high level of repeat enquiries and finds that many of their new users come because the service has been recommended to them by another user.

This is, however, a relatively crude way of measuring whether or not a service is meeting its users' needs. What is actually required is a more systematic approach which monitors the way in which a service is developing and being used and evaluates this against a set of service objectives. This is the approach that we advocated in the planning and evaluation guidelines (Simpkins, 1993).

This approach is fine if the service objectives have been formulated on the basis of a thorough understanding of users' needs. The question is, how can this thorough understanding be arrived at? There is certainly a great deal that can be learned from prior research and from the experience of others who have developed services. There are, however, many who argue that the best way to ensure that service objectives meet the needs of users is to have them established by users.

Certainly information and advice services should be accountable to the communities they serve – if they are not accountable to them then to whom are they accountable? If this accountability is to be a reality, then users should play a key role in the affairs of the service. It is common for disability information and advice services to have constitutions that ensure that they are controlled by disabled people. Six of the NDIP pilot projects chose to have this kind of constitutional arrangement. It is also common for services to be staffed by people who are disabled or by those who have personal experience of disability.

It has to be recognised, however, that such arrangements do not guarantee that the services will meet the needs of the users. A user who becomes a member of a management committee or an advice worker is different from a user who is approaching a service for the first time. This is a general problem and does not relate to disability alone: it is, for example, acknowledged to be a problem with lay representatives on health authorities. All that can be said is that such user representatives are more likely to understand the nature of needs than are many others.

Conclusion

What conclusion can be drawn from the NDIP experience? Do disability information and advice services meet the needs of their users? Do more of them do so now than they did three years ago?

It is, of course, very difficult to come up with meaningful answers to these questions. Some things do, however, seem to be clear. First, there is a greater understanding of the role that disabled people could and should play in the control and operation of disability information and advice services. And it seems probable that more services now have written into their constitutions arrangements that ensure that disabled people are in the majority on management committees.

Secondly, there is a general recognition of the need for careful planning, monitoring and evaluation of services. Only by proceeding in this way is it possible to develop services that respond to users needs. One of the problems faced by the NDIP pilot projects was the fact that the initial proposals had to be prepared very quickly. In a number of cases there was insufficient time for full consultation and for detailed consideration of users needs. Instead service aims and objectives were produced quickly and, in some cases, did not fully take account of the needs of potential users. Some of the projects faced the difficult task of revising their basic aims and objectives during the period of NDIP funding in an attempt to address users' needs more effectively.

Thirdly, there seems to be a better appreciation of the range and nature of subjects that disability information and advice services should cover. And there appears to have been a shift away from a set of priorities based on an individual model of disability – information about impairments, aids and equipment – to a set of priorities that reflects the social model – information on benefits, rights and independent living.

There also appears to be a clearer understanding of the difference between information and advice and, in particular, a recognition that information alone is insufficient to meet the most pressing needs of disabled people.

There is, however, a long delay between the recognition of the need for an active advice service and the development of services that fully meet the need. It is not easy to provide a fully effective advice service. It calls for a considerable amount of experience, skill and a degree of confidence.

Understandably these are not the strongest features of many services that have only recently been established.

In all, it seems that the services have got better at meeting the needs of their users. But we are still a very long way from a position where all the information and advice needs of disabled people are being satisfactorily met.

References

BJM Research Partners (1991) *Department of Social Security information needs*

Berthoud, Richard, Lakey, Jane and McKay, Stephen (1993) *The economic problems of disabled people.* Policy Studies Institute

Bryson, Alex and Kempson, Elaine (1994) *Information and advice about benefits.* Policy Studies Institute

Coopers and Lybrand (1988) *Information needs of disabled people, their carers and service providers.* Department of Health and Social Security

Cragg Ross and Dawson Ltd (1990) *Qualitative assessment of six leaflets*

Craig, Peter (1991) 'Costs and benefits: a review of research on take-up of income-related benefits'. *Journal of Social Policy* 20(4)

Epstein, Joyce (1980) *Information needs of the elderly.* Research Institute for Consumer Affairs

Hasler, Frances (1993) 'The place of information provision in the disability movement' *In: Information enables: improving access to information services for disabled people.* Policy Studies Institute

Hedges, Alan and Ritchie, Jane (1988) *Designing documents for people.* Social and Community Planning Research

Hinkley, Philipa (1992) *The health information needs of senior citizens.* Policy Studies Institute

Kempson, Elaine (1987) *Informing health consumers: a review of consumer health information needs and services.* Consumers Association

Martin, J, White, A and Meltzer, H 1989 *Disabled adults: services, transport and employment* (OPCS Report 4). HMSO

Moore, Nick (1993) 'Information for disabled citizens' *In: Inform '92: meeting the needs of disabled people in Europe.* Department of Health

National Association of Citizens Advice Bureaux (1993) *Working for change: Annual report 1992-93*

National Consumer Council (1977) *The fourth right of citizenship: a review of local advice services*

Office of Population Censuses and Surveys (1988 and 1989) *Reports on disability* (Five reports). HMSO

Perkins Elizabeth, Roberts, Sean and Moore, Nick (1992) *Helping clients claim their benefits: the information needs of informal benefits advisers.* Policy Studies Institute

Prescott-Clarke, P (1990) *Employment and handicap.* Social and Community Planning Research

Simpkins, Rebecca (1993) *Planning and evaluating disability information services.* Policy Studies Institute

Steele, Jane and others (1993) *Informing people about social services.* Policy Studies Institute

Tester, Susan and Meredith (1987) *Ill informed? A study of information and support for elderly people in the inner city.* Policy Studies Institute

12   An adequate supply of appropriate information

There is, in some quarters, an unfortunate tendency to regard information as a 'good thing' – rather like motherhood and brown bread. In such quarters there is a prevailing view that the more information one has, the better. This is to misunderstand the nature of information and the function it performs in daily life.

We have a limited capacity to absorb information and to act on it. Because of this, quality is more important than quantity. What we should strive for is not an unlimited supply of information but an *adequate* supply of *appropriate* information. There should be enough information available to satisfy the immediate need and the information itself should be appropriate in terms of accessibility, relevance, accuracy and currency.

The aim of NDIP was not, therefore, simply to increase the volume of information in circulation, nor was it to encourage the accumulation of large quantities of information in databases or directories. The project sought to ensure first that information was available when and where it was needed; secondly, that it was of acceptable quality and, thirdly, that it was relevant to the range of needs experienced by disabled people.

National information provision
The national provision of information for disabled people is good. National information providers have benefited from the existence of funds under Section 64 of the *Health Services and Public Health Act 1968*. As a result, they now produce an impressive array of information services and products. Certainly, when compared with information and advice provision for other groups within the community, like minority ethnic groups, or subject areas, like housing or employment, the national provision of disability information is very good.

Many organisations are concerned with the provision of information on issues that affect the lives of large numbers of disabled people (Hinkley and Steele, 1992). They are reinforced by very many organisations that are concerned with particular groups of disabled people or with specific impairments or conditions and by providers of generalist information.

Together these bodies produce a substantial amount of information, covering a wide range of subjects. There are no obvious gaps in subject coverage, other than possibly the need to view all issues from the particular perspective of disabled people. Neither is there evidence of unnecessary duplication.

The question of duplication is a difficult one. When resources are limited there is an understandable inclination to reduce duplication as a means of saving money. This can, however, lead to the creation of inefficient monopolies and, more significant, a reduction in consumer choice.

Competition between information providers can generally stimulate the development of better products and services. It can foster innovation; it can encourage information providers to promote their products and services to potential users and it can help to keep costs down.

Users of information also benefit from having a range of products and services to choose from. The information service offered is seldom, if ever, identical. Different providers seek to address different needs. A good example is information about welfare benefits. The Benefits Agency produces a considerable amount of information about disability benefits. The Disability Alliance also provides information about the same benefits yet there are significant real and perceived differences between the two sources. The overall information system would be weakened if one of these information sources were withdrawn in an attempt to reduce duplication.

The markets

National organisations provide information for a range of different markets. We saw in the previous chapter that disabled people, their carers and personal assistants and professionals represented three distinct markets with different needs and expectations. To these we should add local information and advice services. Of these groups, probably the professionals are the best served. They need a continuing flow of information and they can be expected to develop the skills and familiarity necessary to handle sophisticated products and services. They also are in a position where, to a greater or lesser extent, they can buy the information they require. A range of information products and services has been created to meet the professionals' needs. Probably the best example is the information provided by the Disabled Living Foundation.

Disabled people are increasingly recognised as a significant information market. Collectively they generate a very significant demand for information. Yet it is a difficult market to address. For any individual, the information need is intermittent. There is also a severe limitation on the ability of disabled people to contribute to the cost of the information they require.

Carers and personal assistants are, perhaps, the least well provided for. The Carers' National Association has done much to increase awareness of information needs among this group but few information services or products are aimed directly at them.

Local disability information and advice services represent a distinct market that has yet to be fully tapped by the national organisations. There is a growing recognition that national and local information providers form part of the total disability information system and, consequently, they need to work closely together. Local services can use nationally provided information to reinforce and support their advice work. In doing so they can contribute interpretation and, in some cases, the added benefit of direct personal experience to what might otherwise be impersonal and generalised information. Yet the study undertaken by Colin Barnes showed that not many national providers were getting their information through to the local services (Barnes, 1994).

Market research

Few national information providers have undertaken any significant market research. The reasons for this are not difficult to identify. Few national information providers have sufficient spare staff resources to undertake market research and even fewer have sufficient resources to pay others to do it for them. There is, however, a continuing need for national providers to know more about the markets they serve. One exception is the Disabled Living Foundation which undertook a fairly substantial review of the market for its services.

Without such knowledge it is difficult to produce high quality information. The whole question of quality was addressed by a working group established as part of NDIP. This group considered the ways in which national information providers could take steps to improve the quality of their information and, in the longer term, to ensure that quality remains high (Moore, Steele and Boswell, 1994). Its conclusion was that there was a pressing need to give quality a higher priority. This called for a commitment at the highest level, leading to a change in the culture of many organisations and the introduction of quality assurance techniques that could be adopted and 'owned' by the people working day-to-day on the delivery of information. Quality is not a spray-on additive. The concern for quality should permeate all aspects of an organisation.

Funding and pricing

A second working group considered the funding and pricing of information produced at national level. It discovered that few national providers had developed pricing strategies that corresponded to the realities of the markets they were serving. (The funding issues are considered in Chapter 14.) One of the biggest problems is the simple fact that there is insufficient money in the system to enable a conventional market to operate effectively. Most disabled people do not have enough money to pay the full cost of the information they require. Neither do their carers, the professionals or the local information and advice services. So pricing strategies based on market economics are of little value. Most providers base their prices on an imperfect understanding of what the market can bear, combined with a need to conform to a level of prices and expectations set some time in the past. The whole matter is complicated in some organisations by firmly held beliefs that information should be free at the point of use.

The question of pricing is inextricably bound up with the funding of the information system. Only when the system as a whole is adequately resourced will it become possible to allocate information resources on the basis of a pricing structure founded on sound economic principles. Even then it will be desirable to enable disabled people and their carers to obtain information that is free at the point of use (Moore, Steele and Boswell, 1994).

Access

Information is of little value if it cannot be accessed easily by those for whom it is intended. Yet a large amount of the information provided nationally is inaccessible. It is often only available in conventional print form. There is a pressing need for all disability information to be available in Braille, in large print, on computer disc and, in many cases, on audio tape. There is a need for greater use of signers and British Sign Language as well as languages like Makaton that are aimed at people with learning disabilities. There is also a significant need, as the NDIP pilot projects in Oldham, Southwark and Walsall showed, for information to be made available in the languages of the minority ethnic communities.

To provide information in all these different formats is not cheap. It should, however, be regarded as one of the inescapable costs faced by disability information providers.

One way to reduce costs is to make greater use of information technology. Information held in electronic form, for example, can be presented in Braille and large print relatively easily and cheaply if the right equipment is available. There is a need for information providers, both nationally and locally, to invest in the technology that will enable them to present information in different formats.

Technology

There was, at the outset of NDIP, a hope that information and communication technology could be used to create a seamless database of disability information that could be accessed as and when required. This expectation was unrealistic on three principal counts. First there are significant and continuing disparities in the level of technology used by the national information providers. To bring all of them to a common standard would require a significant investment. To raise them all to the level of the most sophisticated – and this is what would be required – would require capital resources beyond anything currently contemplated. Even if the capital resources were available there would be a need for substantial investment in staff training and development and in the re-design of many existing information systems.

The second problem lies at the user end. Very few users have the wherewithal to access such an information system. They may have the basic information technology but for the foreseeable future they lack the necessary skills and the inclination to acquire them. More particularly, they lack the cash resources that would be required to use such a system unless it were heavily subsidised.

Even if these difficulties could be overcome, the task of creating and maintaining such a seamless information system would be organisationally difficult, if not impossible.

We might have expected that, during the three years that NDIP was in existence, we would see advances in the use of information and communications technology by the national providers. In fact the opposite has happened. Developments that were confidently planned in 1991 were shelved or never got beyond the experimental stage and the one online electronic disability information service that existed – DLF Data – has failed to develop as rapidly as was expected. Here the future certainly looks more promising. The current rapid development of low-cost information services over the Internet and other networks offers real possibilities for the electronic dissemination of information.

It is likely, however, that we will look back on this period as a pause in a longer-term process of applying technology to the provision of disability information. The technology continues to develop rapidly. It is becoming much more sophisticated and – even more important – it is becoming dramatically cheaper. There will be a continuing need to monitor this technological development and to encourage its exploitation. Most progress is, however, likely to be made within individual organisations – the single, seamless national information system is still a long way off.

Local information provision

We concluded in the previous chapter that information comes best when wrapped in a knowledgeable person. To that extent, the quality of local information depends greatly on people working in local information and advice services. These people cannot, however, do their job effectively without access to reliable information. They need information that is generated nationally (Barnes, 1994) but they also need a considerable amount of information about local services and circumstances.

Managing local information

Each local service needs to build up a collection of information resources that reflects the aims, objectives and philosophy of the service. In some cases, a local group will base its service on the provision of advice and support services by disabled people for disabled people. In such cases it is possible that the collection and organisation of documentary information will be given a relatively low priority. In other cases, local services give greater emphasis to the provision of information as distinct from advice and here significant resources are likely to be devoted to the collection and organisation of local information. In yet other cases a federation of local information and advice services may have at its heart a unit that collects and organises local information, making it available as a service to the federation members.

There is no single right answer. What is needed is an approach to the management of local information that corresponds to the ethos of the local service. This does not always seem to be the case. There are examples where the desire to build an information collection has shaped the nature of the information and advice service that is offered.

The pilot projects within NDIP offered a range of different approaches to the collection of local information. Some, notably, the Berkshire Disability Information Network, the Devon Disability Information and Advice Federation and the Kent Information Federation, established a central unit to collect, process, and organise local information, in some cases collaborating with local federations or satellites. The resultant databases were then made available as a basic resource to satellite services that were the members of the federation. This enabled the services to avoid duplication and to benefit from a degree of standardisation and the economies of scale.

In other projects the approach was rather different. Here the pilot projects assembled collections of information that were then made available to a relatively wide range of potential users. The Oldham Disability Alliance produced an information pack for use by professionals and also by disabled people, their carers and professional assistants. The pack contains information about local services and resources of interest to disabled people. The Gateshead Disability Information Project responded to a range of perceived needs for disability information and produced two different directories of local services. Again these were made available to a wide range of users within the community. In North East Yorkshire the Information Service collected information and made it available as a database that could be used in general practice surgeries, as information sheets that could be widely distributed and, in Whitby, as an information pack for disabled people, carers and professionals. In Southwark, information packs aimed at disabled people in ethnic minority communities were used as part of a strategy to explore information needs within those communities.

In Gloucester, GUIDE developed a large and relatively sophisticated database of local services and resources. This was used most intensively as the basis for the GUIDE information service. The database was also made available to other users through the health authority information networks and as a database that could be mounted on stand-alone personal computers.

In Manchester, the Disability Information Service considered the possibility of collecting local disability information but decided that there were already a number of groups doing just that. Instead it decided to provide a referral service and consequently built up a collection of information about other sources of information and advice for disabled people. Birmingham Information Federation adopted a similar approach with its LinkLine.

In Norfolk, the Disability Information Federation was asked by the local authority to develop a database of information about services and resources for disabled people that could be incorporated on the county videotex information system. The need to respond positively to a potential funder led to a reinterpretation of the federation's aims and objectives and, as a result, a different form of federation service emerged, largely based around the development of a database that could be made available to local groups. Previously, the emphasis was much more on strengthening and supporting the development of local groups concerned with information provision for disabled people.

There is clearly a wide range of approaches that can be adopted towards the management of local information. A number of issues need to be considered.

Information and advice

First, there is the question of the balance between information and advice. Our analysis of information needs (Chapter 11) suggests that there the most significant needs are for advice on issues like benefits, income maintenance, housing and employment. Relatively little local information is required to meet these needs for advice. Advisers need access to nationally produced information like the Disability Alliance's *Disability rights handbook* and they need to establish a working relationship with staff in the local office of the Benefits Agency, the housing department and the Employment Service. But they need relatively little other information. What *is* needed is training and experience.

It is important, therefore, to keep the collection, organisation and management of information in proportion and to ask periodically whether the resources devoted to these tasks could be better used in other ways.

This is self-evident yet it is an issue that seldom seems to be addressed. It is also the case that information collection is a 'safe' activity. If one is unsure of one's ability to deal with acute problems like a person's failure to obtain the benefits to which they feel they are entitled; if one is unsure about how to begin operating an information and advice service that will meet the needs of an ill-defined community; if one's management committee is sending out conflicting signals about the nature of the service to be offered, then one feels safe in being busy collecting information and in building up a database even if relatively little use is made of the end product.

Frequency of need

Another question to be addressed is the balance between investing effort in the collection of information *in anticipation of a need* as distinct from collecting it *in response to a demand*. If it is possible to predict with some certainty that an item of information will be required frequently, then it makes sense to collect the information in advance and to hold it so that it can be accessed easily whenever it is needed. If, however, it is not possible to predict demand in that way, then it may be more effective to collect the information only when someone needs it. Otherwise one runs the risk of spending time and effort collecting information that will not be used. A useful check is to record on the database when an item of information is used and to review periodically how much of the collection is being used.

For example, all disability information and advice services should have easily accessible the current benefit rates that relate to disabled people and the name of the person in the local office of the Benefits Agency that deals with enquiries about the main disability benefits. It is possible to predict with some confidence that this information will be needed frequently. On the other hand it is not possible to predict whether there will be a demand for information about a day centre at the other end of the county. If such a demand arises it would not be difficult to use the telephone to find out the necessary information there and then.

Local databases should, in general, only contain information for which there is a reasonably predictable demand.

Currency

This raises a further issue – that of currency. Out-of-date information is seldom of value. In some circumstances it can be positively unhelpful. There is, therefore a pressing need to keep a collection of local information up-to-date. This can be a time-consuming task and it is one of the reasons why it makes sense to share the collection and up-dating of information or to centralise it in the central unit of a federation. Each item of information should be regarded as having a 'use-by' date attached to it. One implication of this is that the question of likely use then becomes 'is this information likely to be used before is passes its use-by date?'

Quality

Currency is an aspect of quality. But it is not the only thing that determines quality in a local information collection. Other dimensions of quality concern coverage and comprehensiveness; ease of retrieval; ease of use once retrieved and relevance to the task in hand. It is not possible to achieve a high level of quality on these counts without making a particular effort. Just as with the national information providers, it is necessary to build a concern for quality into all aspects and levels of the service.

Consideration of these issues tends to suggest that far from the problem being the lack of local information, the real problem may well be that too many resources are being devoted to its collection.

Retrieval

The classification and organisation of information is important. If information is not organised effectively there is a risk that pieces of information will become lost or that staff will fail to retrieve the information they need to answer an enquiry. The Disability Information Service in Surrey (DISS) has developed a classification scheme to organise its

131

collection of information about disability. In 1992 DISS made the scheme available to other groups and services (Disability Information Service in Surrey, 1992). The scheme was taken up by a number of groups but rejected by others.

Within NDIP there was a clearly articulated demand for a classification scheme that could be used by a wide variety of groups and which could also be accepted as a standard that national providers could use to pre-classify their information. The DISS scheme appeared to offer the best prospect and a small study was launched to evaluate how the scheme was being used, to obtain users' views on the ways in which it could be improved and to assess why some groups had rejected it. The study was carried out by staff from the University of Central England (Nankivell and Brown, 1994). During the course of the work a number of other classification schemes were identified and these were compared against the DISS scheme.

The conclusion of the study was that, while the DISS scheme had a number of drawbacks, particularly its perceived foundation in the medical rather than the social model of disability, it offered the best prospect for development as a scheme that could be nationally applicable. To give effect to this, DISS has established a user group to provide feedback and to make suggestions about ways in which the scheme can be improved.

The DISS scheme was evaluated in terms of its use as a tool for organising collections of documents. There is also a need for something to organise information in a computer database. This can be a classification scheme like DISS, but there are other possibilities, notably thesauri which are controlled lists of terms that are used as keywords in identifying documents or pieces of information (the GUIDE service developed a thesaurus for its database (GUIDE, 1993)). While not originally designed for a database, the DISS scheme can be used for this purpose. (Computer databases are discussed in more detail in Chapter 16.)

DISS is one of a number of organisations that produce an information service aimed specifically at local disability information and advice agencies. It provides a computer-based system that contains all the national information contained in the DISS database in Surrey. Along with this information the local service gets the software needed to search and retrieve the information. It is also possible to purchase software that will enable the local service to incorporate local information in the database. A similar service is offered by a number of other organisations, notably GUIDE and INCHES in Cheshire.

Other organisations provide paper-based information services for local groups. Age Concern, DIAL UK, MIND, RADAR and others each supply a regular flow of information to their member groups. DIAL UK is exploring the scope for providing this in electronic form as well as on paper.

Conclusion

We have to recognise that managing a collection of information in a local disability information and advice centre is not an easy task. It is time-consuming and it is a job that calls for a particular range of skills and abilities. Also, while computer-based systems offer great improvements in the ability to store, update and retrieve information, their introduction can be a complex matter. All the pilot projects in NDIP found that they spent longer than expected building up and maintaining their information collections. Those that introduced computer-systems found that it was an extremely time-consuming task.

The lesson for others embarking on the development of local information collections is to think long and hard about the balance between collecting information in advance of an enquiry and collecting it in response to a demand. And only to commit resources to information *collection* when one is certain that the effort will directly support the information and advice *provision* work of the service.

References

Barnes, Colin (1994) *From national to local: an evaluation of the effectiveness of national disablement information providers' services to local disablement information services.* British Council of Organisations of Disabled People

Disability Information Service in Surrey (1992) *Classification scheme*

GUIDE (1993) *Thesaurus of disability terms*

Hinkley, Philipa and Steele, Jane (1992) *National disability information provision: sources and issues.* Policy Studies Institute

Moore, Nick, Steele, Jane and Boswell, Caroline (1994) *Improving the provision of national disability information.* Policy Studies Institute

Nankivell, Claire and Pauline Brown (1994) *Can the DISS classification scheme be developed for national use?* University of Central England

13   An even pattern of provision

Disabled people live in all parts of the country: in suburbia, inner cities and in rural areas. Consequently, information and advice services need to be provided in all parts of the country. At the beginning of NDIP, however, relatively little was known about the distribution of services.

The initial call for proposals to become pilot projects within NDIP generated nearly 100 responses from all parts of the country. But when we surveyed these applicants six months later we found that only about one third were still in existence as federations (Simpkins and Nadash, 1993). We felt it was important, therefore, to find out more about the actual pattern of provision.

To do this we compiled a directory of local disability information and advice services (Nadash, 1993). The basis for this was a survey of over 1,400 local groups and providers from which we were able to identify nearly 600 agencies that were providing an information and advice service aimed directly at disabled people and their carers.

Information and advice is available from a range of sources and it is important to be clear about what we define as a local disability information provider.

> We tried to restrict entries in the directory to those groups that could provide information on a wide range of disability issues, or that focused on information which was likely to be relevant to most disabled people. So, on this basis, groups which were concerned with particular impairments were excluded, as were groups which were concerned with access (Nadash, 1993).

The exceptions were local groups of Age Concern, MIND and Mencap as they provide information and advice on a range of topics – to a significant proportion of the disabled population.

We excluded generalist advice providers like citizens advice bureaux unless they employed specialist disability advice workers. We also excluded health, housing and employment information services and grassroots disability rights or campaigning groups except where these groups offered a specific information and advice service.

We were, therefore, attempting to identify the main local disability information and advice services, although we recognise that they are supported by a large number of other groups and services that provide information.

The first thing to emerge from the directory was the large number of services that we were able to identify. We expected to find about 300 services and were surprised to discover twice as many. What we were not able to discover was whether the number of services was growing and, if so, at what rate. The impression that we formed while collecting the information was that a significant proportion of the services were quite new and that the publicity associated with NDIP had served to stimulate the development of new services. There are plans to up-date the directory and this should provide an indication of the rate of growth.

The second striking thing was the relatively even distribution across the country. Services were provided in all counties, in Greater London and in the metropolitan areas. Not surprisingly, most were located in centres of population, although a number clearly sought to provide services in relatively sparsely populated rural areas.

A few services appeared to operate entirely independently. Most, however, had some links with other groups. A large number were part of national networks. We have already mentioned Age Concern, MIND and Mencap. The other national networks represented were RADAR, DIAL UK and FIAC — the Federation of Independent Information and Advice Centres. Membership of such national networks clearly brings with it opportunities to receive nationally generated information as well as training and other general support.

Other services were members of local federations. As we showed in Chapter Nine, these federations vary considerably in their approach and structure. It was, however, encouraging to see that within geographical areas, local services were coming together to share information and expertise.

The impression given by the information collected for the directory was positive. There exists a network of local services that can do much to meet the need for information and advice among disabled people. Undoubtedly that network can be strengthened – both in terms of increasing the number and strengthening individual services – but the basic framework exists.

Provision and need

We need to ask whether the existing pattern of provision is sufficient to meet the need for information and advice. One way to do this is to look at general standards for the provision of advice services. The mostly generally accepted advice service standards were drawn up by the National Consumer Council in 1986 (National Consumer Council, 1986). (The standards are currently under review but the results have not yet been published.)

Good advice for all recommends that there should be one generalist advice worker for every 4,000 members of the population. It notes, however, that areas with a high incidence of low incomes need more generous provision. It is well known that disabled people have below-average incomes (Office of Population Censuses and Surveys, 1988 and 1989), so it might be reasonable to expect that the ratio of advice workers to members of the disabled population might need to be 1:3000.

There are estimated to be 6.9 million disabled adults in Great Britain (Berthoud, Lakey and McKay, 1993) and 360,000 disabled children (Office of Population Censuses and Surveys 1988 and 1989) whose parents might need specialist disability information and advice. This gives a total of 7.26 million disabled people in Great Britain. The equivalent figure for England is 6.17 million. The standards suggest that just over 2,000 generalist information and advice workers will be needed to provide the basic minimum level of advice for disabled people.

Good advice for all goes on to recommend that there should be a minimum number of three staff in each advice centre. This minimum of three is needed to enable the centre to remain open during staff holidays, periods of illness, training and so on. On this basis we would need about 670 properly staffed disability information and advice centres to meet the needs of the disabled population in England. The NDIP directory shows that we are close to having that number of information and advice centres. There is some doubt, however, about the adequacy of their staffing levels.

We did not collect information about staffing levels when compiling the directory. It seems unlikely, however, that many of the centres included in the directory have the equivalent of three full-time staff.

On the basis of this analysis, the priority should be to strengthen the existing network of local services. There is a residual need to increase the size of the network by establishing new centres but future development efforts should focus on increasing the resources available for the services that currently exist.

References

Berthoud, Richard, Lakey, Jane and McKay, Stephen (1993) *The economic problems of disabled people.* Policy Studies Institute

Nadash, Pamela (1993) *Directory of local disability information providers.* Policy Studies Institute

National Consumer Council (1986) *Good advice for all: guidelines on standards for local advice services*

Office of Population Censuses and Surveys (1988 and 1989) *Reports on disability* (Five reports). HMSO

Simpkins, Rebecca and Nadash, Pamela (1993) *Disability information federations: features and issues*. Policy Studies Institute

14　An adequate and stable source of funding

The general development of advice services in Britain has been limited by inadequate and unreliable funding. If we are to develop a reliable disability information and advice system we must take steps to ensure that there is an adequate and stable source of funding. The signs are, however, far from promising.

Funding at national level
We have seen in Chapter Eight that the national information providers are heavily dependent on grants made by the Department of Health under Section 64 of the *Health Services and Public Health Act 1968*. We also saw that the changes in the principles governing these grants have introduced additional uncertainty into the system. In essence the government is changing the system from one which used to contribute to the core costs of organisations to one which focuses on innovative and developmental projects. The long-term impact of these changes could be very significant.

A number of questions needed to be considered. First, is the funding adequate? Are sufficient resources being committed to the production of disability information at a national level? Is the balance between national and local funding about right? Secondly, are there alternative ways of funding national provision? Thirdly, are the funding arrangements stable enough to encourage long-term growth and development?

Levels of funding
The question of the adequacy of the funding is difficult to answer satisfactorily. It is in the nature of things that people feel that current levels of funding are inadequate. They are conscious of what could be achieved if they had more resources. In many cases they are also squeezing as much as is possible out of the resources at their disposal. So one might expect that national information providers would be able to make a good case for additional resources. This case was, indeed, made in the NDIP Working

Group on the funding and pricing of national disability information (Moore, Steele and Boswell, 1994). It is, however, necessary to take a broader view.

First, it should be recognised that national disability information provision is relatively well-resourced compared to, for example, information about welfare benefits or information about housing rights. A number of disability organisations receive direct financial support to enable them to generate information and this is not generally the case in other subject areas. This does not necessarily mean that national disability information providers receive too much financial help from the government – it probably reflects more on the depressingly low levels of funding elsewhere. Moreover, other issues need to be taken into account. In an area like employment rights, for example, other factors mitigate the need for central government support. A great deal of information is made available by trades unions and professional associations for their members. There is also a more discernible market for information products and, consequently, a number of commercial publishers produce relevant information.

We should also recognise that the government provides a considerable amount of support for the generalist information and advice function – in 1992-93, for example, the Department of Trade and Industry grant to the National Association of Citizens Advice Bureaux amounted to £11.4 million. This was for central services such as the provision of information, training and consultancy services. This enables NACAB to provide the equivalent of over £10,000 worth of services for each bureau in membership. In the same year the Department of Health grant to DIAL UK, the equivalent organisation in the disability advice field, was £45,000. Using this money DIAL UK was able to provide the equivalent of about £450 worth of services for each DIAL in membership.

So, while on first glance it may appear that national providers of disability information do well out of the Section 64 funds, the reality is rather different.

Balance of funding

Secondly, we need to consider whether the balance of funding between national and local providers is about right – if more resources became available for the system as a whole, would they generate greater benefits if they were given to national providers or local providers? Here the answer was a little clearer. The consensus among the members of the working group – who represented both national and local information services – was that, on balance, the need for additional resources was greatest among the local services. Although, again, this needs to be seen in the context of the very low levels of funding received by most local disability information and advice services.

There is also the question of the balance of funding between national providers. The incremental nature of funding schemes like Section 64 means that organisations that have been in the scheme from an early stage receive larger amounts of support than do comparable organisations that entered the scheme later. One effect of the current revision of the Section 64 arrangements is to make it more feasible to break out of this historical pattern and to base the allocation of resources more closely on need. It has to be recognised, however, that this means that some well-established national information providers face reductions in the level of financial support that they have been receiving.

The unavoidable conclusion is that there are insufficient resources in the system as a whole. The national information providers have received valuable support in the past through Section 64 grants and they are relatively well-funded in comparison to local services. The level of support is not, however, generous and there are many pressing demands that could be satisfied if additional funds were available.

Alternative sources

The question of alternative sources of funding is a perennial one. All the national information providers face the need to seek funds from elsewhere. The difficulty is that the alternative sources prove elusive.

One obvious possibility is to generate income through the sale of publications or through charged-for information and advisory services. Most national information providers raise some income in this way but they face quite severe limitations. The main limiting factor is the lack of purchasing power in the system. We have already seen that disabled people and their carers have lower than average incomes and, if faced with the need to pay for the information they require, many would be forced to go without. Professionals are in a better position to pay but many of them face reduced budgets – the lack of funds was the most frequently cited reason why professionals cancelled their subscriptions to the DLF information service, for example. The other potential source of sales is local information and advice services but, as Colin Barnes showed, very few have sufficient resources to buy even the most basic set of information (Barnes, 1994).

National information providers are, understandably, reluctant to levy charges that may prevent potential users of their services from gaining access to the information they need. Indeed, most of the providers are charities, the aim of which is to meet information and other needs, not to make money through sales.

A second potential source of funding is through sponsorship and donations. The scope is limited here too. One limitation is the fact that donors seldom want to become committed to long-term financial support for core activities. They are more attracted to innovative demonstration projects – just the kind of project that the revised Section 64 is seeking to support. It is also often difficult to persuade donors to support something as intangible as an information service. Corporate donors in the private sector understandably want something in return for their donation. In some cases printing the company name and logo on a publication will be sufficient reward but, for many companies, such benefits are not sufficient to justify a donation.

The range of alternative sources of funding in the public sector is also limited. There is a small number European Union programmes like TIDE that could potentially offer financial support. But they tend to focus on the innovative demonstration projects and they are seldom available for an organisation's core costs. There are few, if any, sources within the British public sector.

The inescapable conclusion is that the Department of Health is and will continue to be the most significant source of financial support for the national provision of disability information whether under Section 64 or by some other means.

Stable funding

The third set of issues concerns the stability of funding. In Britain the voluntary sector is made inherently unstable by the short-term commitment offered by funders. Very few voluntary bodies are able to rely on funding commitments that stretch beyond the end of the current financial year. In times of prosperity, when there is a good chance that grants will be renewed, the impact of this short-term funding is ameliorated. When national political and economic conditions are less favourable the whole voluntary sector becomes very unstable. National information providers suffer along with the rest. Here it has to be recognised, however, that the Section 64 grants are normally given for three years, although increasingly they are tapered so that the amount given reduces each year. This gives the national information providers a some degree of stability.

This instability carries with it real costs. It leads to loss of efficiency and the kind of sub-optimal performance that results from a failure to undertake long-term planning. It is seldom possible to offer staff anything longer than a twelve-month employment contract. And frequently voluntary organisations have to issue staff with redundancy notices towards the end of each financial year. Understandably, this is unsettling. It has an impact both on recruitment and on retention with a resultant loss of skills and expertise. Neither is it possible to undertake developmental activities that extend beyond the end of the current financial year, unless funding is guaranteed.

Short-term funding carries with it another cost – the cost of seeking alternative sources of funding, or additional funds to make good a shortfall brought about by tapering funding. Time spent seeking these resources could be better spent providing services.

There is a real need to reduce the level of instability and uncertainty that is inherent in the current system for providing financial support to national information providers. Yet the changes to the Section 64 arrangements have served to increase rather than to reduce the level of instability.

The case for government funding

A strong case can be made for government support of national information provision. First, national information providers are in a position to benefit from economies of scale and to reduce unnecessary duplication in the collection of information. The economies of scale come simply from the national level of operation. Because the volume of information being processed is great the national information providers are able to develop specialist skills, to take advantage of information technology, and to introduce systems that reduce the unit cost of processing information. They are also in a position where they can collect the information once and make that information available to a large number of users who would otherwise have to collect it for themselves. It clearly would not make sense, for example, for every occupational therapist and disability information centre to attempt to collect all the information they needed from wheelchair suppliers. It is much more sensible to have one or two organisations collecting the information and making it generally available.

The government also benefits from the information activity. The government needs effective information services to inform people about the complex society that we inhabit. In recent years the need for these services has been recognised in a series of citizens charters. The government needs to be able to inform people about their rights, entitlements and responsibilities. A certain amount can be achieved through official channels. Some official bodies, like the Benefits Agency, give a high priority to the communication of information about their activities, yet there is a clear need for other information services to supplement the official organs. Such alternative sources also help to make the system function effectively by helping people negotiate with the official bodies. Both the individual and the DSS benefits when a local information centre, perhaps using information from the *Disability rights handbook*, helps a disabled person make a claim for a disability benefit.

The state also benefits through receiving feedback about the consequences and effects of its legislation. The Benefits Agency has recognised this and has established a formal consultation process with representatives of advice services to receive feedback.

Government departments, in particular the Department of Health, have therefore a continuing role to play in the support of national disability information provision. There is a need to increase the level of support. There is also currently a pressing need to review the changes that have taken place with Section 64 and to reconsider the long-term consequences of the new arrangements.

Funding at local level
The difficulties faced by national providers are magnified at the local level. There are insufficient funds currently going into the system. They are inherently unstable and there are few alternative sources of support.

The twelve NDIP pilot projects were relatively well-funded. The amounts they received each year to cover revenue expenditure ranged from £36,000 to over £80,000. This compares with the average grant for a local DIAL group of £13,500. So the experience of the NDIP pilot projects was not typical. Most local disability information and advice services have a hand-to-mouth existence, providing services from a very low level of support.

One consequence of this is the need to rely heavily on volunteers. Information and advice services are, by their very nature, labour-intensive. The major cost of a properly funded service is staffing. Currently volunteer workers in disability information and advice services are providing a very considerable subsidy for a service that meets significant social needs.

As part of NDIP we reviewed the sources of financial support available to local disability information and advice services (Shiner, 1993). This review showed that local authorities continue to be the most obvious source of funds, followed by health authorities. Other sources, such as central government departments, the European Commission, charitable trusts and company donations are relatively insignificant.

Local authorities
Local authorities have a number of statutory duties to provide information relevant to disabled people. *The Chronically Sick and Disabled Persons Act 1970* required social services departments to publish information about

services that were known to them 'from time to time'. *The Disabled Persons Act 1986* requires each local authority to ensure that disabled people using its services were informed about other relevant services. *The Local Government and Housing Act 1989* empowers local authorities to fund voluntary organisations that give advice and assistance to people concerning their rights and obligations.

The most significant duties to inform have been placed on local authorities by *The NHS and Community Care Act 1990*. This Act requires local authorities to publish information accessible to all potential service users and carers, including those with any communication difficulty, setting out the types of community care service available. It also requires local authorities to publish their community care plans and these plans should set out their proposals for informing people about the services offered. Local information and advice services therefore have a basis for applying for financial support and they also have the means of influencing the way that the local authority will support information activities.

In addition to these statutory duties, local authorities have been encouraged through official circulars and guidance to make information available on a substantial range of community care topics (Steele and others, 1993).

Many local authorities have readily accepted their responsibility for supporting local information and advice initiatives. Most local advice centres receive the bulk of their funds from the local authority – citizens advice bureaux, neighbourhood advice centres, housing aid centres, even some law centres. Some local authorities, notably Leicester, Manchester, Oldham and Thamesdown, have gone much further and have worked with local advice services to draw up a strategic development plan for the services.

One of the important aspects of this support is the recognition of the need for independence. Advice services are frequently called upon to act on behalf of an individual in their dealings with the local authority. If they are to do this successfully they need to be independent of the authority. Most local authorities recognise this and fulfil their general responsibilities to provide information and advice by supporting independently managed services in the voluntary sector.

There is increasing evidence to show that social services departments are adopting a similar stance in relation to their responsibilities under *The NHS and Community Care Act*. In Gateshead, for example, the health commission and the local authority jointly issued a contract to the Gateshead Council on Disability and the Libraries and Arts Service (the two host organisations for GDIP) to provide a Community Care

Information Service, while in Norfolk the county council has contracted with the Norfolk Disability Information Federation to supply information about services and facilities for disabled people for inclusion on the county database. A similar approach has been adopted by Devon County Council which has been a strong supporter of the Devon Disability Information and Advice Federation. In several other NDIP pilot projects, such as Kent, North East Yorkshire and Oldham the local authority has contributed significantly to the development of the information and advice services.

It has to be recognised, however, that it is much easier to persuade local and health authorities to fund an activity that generates a tangible service or product. The NDIP pilot projects have shown that it is easier, for example, to obtain funding for a database or to support a direct public service than it is to obtain funding for developmental and support services.

There is undoubtedly much more that can be achieved in the future. But it is not all entirely straightforward. The relationship between the local authority and the voluntary sector information and advice service is not always an easy one to manage. There is an acknowledged need for services to be independently managed but there is an equally understandable desire on the part of a funder to have some say in how the money is spent. It is no more, nor less than the tensions between purchasers and providers that exist within the newly reorganised social services departments and health services. As time goes on, no doubt the respective roles will become more clearly established.

One way of managing the relationship is to codify the terms of the financial support in the form of a contract or service-level agreement. These agreements are steadily replacing the old system of grant aid where a voluntary sector body applied each year to the local authority for a grant which was usually based on what they got last year plus as much extra as they thought they could reasonably justify. The service level agreement, in contrast, specifies more precisely what services and activities will be provided in return for the financial support. It provides a more businesslike basis for the relationship between the funder and the voluntary sector – defining the relationship so that it more closely resembles the purchaser–provider relationship that underpins the NHS and community care reforms. Of perhaps greater significance is the fact that some service-level agreements extend over more than one financial year and thus offer the prospect of reducing the uncertainty in the system.

This move towards service-level agreements has not been universally welcomed by the voluntary sector. Many feel that it increases the degree of accountability to the funder at the expense of accountability to the service users. It can also lead to unnecessarily complex administrative routines and data collection exercises in order to provide the funder with the information required to monitor the terms of the contract. The opposing view is that the service-level agreements are helping to inject a degree of management and efficiency that has long been overdue. Local authorities also point out with some justification that they represent the interests of users.

Whichever view prevails, it seems likely that service-level agreements will become more, rather than less, common in the future and the voluntary sector bodies that will benefit most will be those that most quickly come to terms with this new way of managing the relationship between funder and service provider.

Health authorities

Health authorities are the second most significant source of financial assistance for disability information and advice services. But here the situation is complex and volatile. The health sector is continuing to undergo fundamental change and it is difficult to predict what the outcome will be for disability information and advice services. The main change is the introduction of the split between purchasers and providers. The question for disability information and advice services is: which side of the relationship is the likely funder of information and advice services? In one sense it is the purchasers. Their job is to buy health services on behalf of their local population. To that extent, they have a role in buying information and advice services to support the health care. On the other hand, the providers seek to deliver the best possible service, or at least the service that is most attractive to the purchasers. There is a case to be made for them supporting information and advice services as a desirable adjunct to their basic provision.

No-one has yet clearly established the answer. At the moment, the best prospects appear to lie with applications to the purchasers.

For many groups, of course, there is a major problem with seeking support from the health service. Put simply, it tends to emphasise the medical model of disability at a time when many groups are seeking to change people's perceptions and to base services on a social model.

Joint finance

The government makes available money that can be used for schemes initiated jointly by health and local authorities. In part the scheme is intended to assist the changes in the relationships between health and community care services. The funds are managed by joint consultative groups which often include representatives from the voluntary sector and in a number of cases they have been used to support disability information and advice services. The GUIDE service in Gloucester was established in 1990 with funds from joint finance which gave a commitment to provide core funding for seven years. The Berkshire Disability Information Network received valuable financial support from joint finance to supplement the NDIP funding. In Somerset the Disability Information Federation has been supported from the outset by joint finance and has used the funds to establish a robust network of services within the county.

Other sources

There is a variety of other potential sources of funds available to support local disability information and advice services. There are charitable trusts and foundations, private sector donors, central government schemes like the City Challenge and, as always, the prospect of a pot of gold in the European Commission.

In his research for the guidelines on fundraising, Michael Shiner was unable to identify very few services that raised significant funds from these sources (Shiner, 1993). Some had been able to raise money from private companies or from charitable trusts but the sums were small, particularly in relation to the time and effort needed to raise them.

Conclusion

So it seems that local authorities and joint finance are the principal sources of funds for local disability information and advice services. How much should they be expecting to pay for these services?

We have seen that the NDIP pilot projects were funded at a higher level than many others. Was that level realistic? Or is the average amount awarded to local DIALs – £13,500 a year – a more accurate guide? To answer this question we can turn again to the National Consumer Standards (National Consumer Council, 1986).

Based on these standards, a town with a population of 50,000, including about 6,500 disabled people, requires the equivalent of two full-time disability information and advice workers. Using average salaries within the voluntary sector, and making the necessary allowances for accommodation and other overhead expenses, it would cost slightly more than £50,000 to meet the basic need for information and advice among the disabled community within that town. The equivalent total cost for a county with a population of 400,000 would be in the order of £450,000 although that cost would almost certainly be shared between the county and district councils.

Few disability information and advice services are funded at anything like this level.

We face, therefore, a significant shortfall between the amount needed to provide a basic disability information and advice service at local level and the amount that is currently being made available. The greatest challenge facing the developers of information and advice services for disabled people is the need to raise substantially the resources available for these services.

References

Barnes, Colin (1994) *From national to local: an evaluation of the effectiveness of national disablement information providers' services to local disablement information providers.* British Council of Organisations of Disabled People

Moore, Nick, Steele, Jane and Boswell, Caroline (1994) *Improving the national provision of disability information.* Policy Studies Institute

National Consumer Council (1986) *Good advice for all: guidelines on standards for local advice services.*

Shiner, Michael (1993) *Fundraising: sources and skills for disability information services.* Policy Studies Institute

Steele, Jane, Hinkley, Philipa, Rowlands, Ian and Moore, Nick (1993) *Informing people about social services: summary of legislation and guidance.* Policy Studies Institute

15 Well-trained and well-paid staff

Information and advice services are labour-intensive. They call for a high level of subject knowledge and an equally high level of skill. It is important that all staff working in disability information and advice services are well trained. It is also important that they are well paid.

As we have seen in Chapter 13, we need about 2,000 information and advice workers to meet the basic needs among the community of disabled people. There are no statistics to show how many information and advice workers there are but it seems likely that there is a considerable shortfall. Certainly few of the 600 or so disability information and advice services that we identified have more than three full-time equivalent staff. There is, therefore a need to increase the number of information and advice workers. We need to consider what kind of skills these workers should have.

The skills that are required

Staff working in disability information and advice services need skills in four different areas: advice work; information work; disability awareness and management.

Advice work

Advice work calls for two essentials – a thorough understanding of the subject and good inter-personal skills. Subject knowledge is essential. People using an advice service are seeking expertise and a high level of understanding. Much will depend on their perception of the expertise of the adviser. If they do not trust the adviser they are unlikely to act on the information and advice given. No-one expects advice workers to memorise the details of benefit rates, eligibility rules, or the details of community care facilities. What they do expect is a thorough understanding of the ways in which the systems operate, what the basic rules are and how to retrieve the detailed information quickly and efficiently. There is, consequently, a continuing need for training in the subjects that are most frequently dealt with by the information and advice service.

Inter-personal skills are equally important. Advisers have to deal with people who are frequently in a distressed state. Their problems can be very pressing and, in some cases, they may be bewildered by the complexities of systems that they do not understand. A good advice worker will inspire trust and confidence. They will be able to establish a rapport with the client and will be able to initiate a dialogue that will go beyond the immediate issue to identify any underlying problems that need to be sorted out. At the same time they must be able to distance themselves from the often distressing problems that they have to deal with. This is not easy. A few services, such as the Help for Health – the telephone-based consumer health information service – have taken steps to ensure that staff have access to counselling and support services to help them cope with the after-effects of stressful enquiries.

Advice workers also need good negotiation skills to enable them to act on behalf of clients in their dealings with service providers. Just as they have to inspire trust in their clients so, too, do they have to inspire confidence in the people with whom they are negotiating.

Some information and advice workers are called upon to represent their clients at tribunals and at appeals proceedings. This calls for very well-developed presentational and negotiating skills linked to a very thorough understanding of the subject.

Most of the national networks of advice services provide training in these areas. Indeed, access to this training is one of the main benefits that can come from membership of these networks.

Information skills

In Chapter 12 we commented on the range of skills needed to manage information in a disability information and advice centre. These skills include the ability to collect information, to organise, store, retrieve and update it. To these can be added the need to be able to exploit information technology and to publish and disseminate information.

Collecting information calls for a degree of judgement. It is not simply a question of sending a questionnaire to all day centres in the vicinity. Such activity should be preceded by an analysis of the service's needs to establish whether or not the information is actually required. This selection of information sources is all the more important when the amount of money available for information is limited.

Organising information can be a very complex task. Even if an information and advice service decides to use one of the generally available classification schemes, like that produced by the Disability Information Service in Surrey, there are many areas where allocation decisions need to be made. There is also a need for consistency and for documenting decisions so that items of information on the same subject end up in the same place or are allocated the same keywords.

Storing information these days usually involves the use of some form of computer database. A range of such systems is available (See Chapter 16). Even with these, however, it requires a degree of skill to apply them successfully.

The art of retrieving information lies in the ability to conduct a search that retrieves just the right amount of relevant information. It is usually easy to retrieve everything that has a bearing on the subject. It is often just as easy to retrieve a single relevant item. It is more difficult to achieve the right balance so that the single relevant item is put into a broader context. What is more, retrieval should be quick and reliable.

Updating skills depend on an awareness of the fact that most information deteriorates over time. Some information remains valid for a certain period then changes suddenly – benefit rates are a good example. Other items of information deteriorate more gradually. A good information and advice worker should be aware of these deterioration rates and should act accordingly, checking information that seems suspect.

We have already referred to information technology skills. Such technology is becoming more and more common and, while it is true that the systems are becoming easier to use, they are becoming more and more sophisticated. It is not possible simply to assume that workers will be happy retrieving information from databases, using electronic mail and so on.

Finally skills are needed in the communication and dissemination of information. Many good information and advice services publish newsletters, fact-sheets and other publications – the range of such publications produced by the NDIP projects was impressive. To make these publications effective calls for a range of information design skills.

In addition to all these skills, good information workers need to be systematic, to pay attention to detail and to be obsessive about checking the accuracy of information.

Disability awareness

Information and advice workers in services aimed at disabled people clearly need to be aware of the particular needs and circumstances of disabled people.

Many would argue that what is actually needed is personal experience of disability. Only with this personal experience does it become possible to empathise with the service's clients. Such personal experience is clearly essential if the service is seeking to meet the need for what Frances Hasler has called information about 'how to live and how to participate as equal citizens' (Hasler, 1993).

Management skills

Disability information and advice services are usually freestanding organisations that have to rely on their own resources for all their management and administration. Sometimes they are set up as part of, or under the umbrella of, a larger organisation. More usually they are like small businesses. As such they need to be managed and administered effectively. This calls for its own set of skills.

Those who manage disability information and advice services need access to skills in financial planning and management, monitoring and service evaluation, personnel administration and management and in negotiating with funders and other external organisations.

This need for management skill is common throughout the voluntary sector and there is a wide range of courses available in most parts of the country.

The importance of personality

One clear lesson from the NDIP experience was that personality was a critical factor in determining the progress and impact of a service.

The ideal worker in a disability information and advice service should be outward-looking; confident in their own abilities; cheerful and constructive; a natural team-worker; reliable and prepared to turn their hand to anything. Clearly, such people are few and far between but their presence in a disability information and advice service can make a very significant difference.

The role of volunteers

Volunteers have played an important part in the development of information and advice services. In many services they continue to make a valued contribution to the work of the agency. Their role does, however, need to be considered carefully.

First, there is a danger of over-reliance. It is easy to establish a service based on the enthusiastic commitment of a small number of volunteers. The long-term maintenance of a service on such a basis is a different matter. People move on and active volunteers often find their interests taking them in different directions. It is all too easy to find what started as a vigorous service breaking down because key volunteers have channelled their energies elsewhere.

Secondly, it is not always easy to recruit suitable volunteers. There is a strong case to be made for treating the recruitment of volunteers as seriously as the recruitment of paid staff. They should have job descriptions, should be recruited through public advertisement, they should be interviewed and, if successful, given a contract that clearly specifies what is expected of them. Only in this way is it possible to ensure that the service is staffed by appropriate individuals who have the skills and experience required. What needs to be remembered is the fact that users will depend on the service for help to sort out crucial problems and they have a right to expect that they will be dealt with by a properly skilled and experienced worker – whether volunteer or paid.

Recruited volunteers often move on after a short time. Many will, quite rightly, regard their volunteer work as a means of gaining or regaining a place in the paid labour force. It is to be expected that they will use the training and experience they have gained to improve their employment prospects. It follows that the better the training and the work experience, the greater will be the turnover. This can make the use of volunteers a costly option.

Many potential volunteers will be dependent on benefits. Care needs to be taken to ensure that their voluntary work does not jeopardise their entitlement to benefit.

There is also a danger that initial over-reliance on volunteers obscures from funders the real costs of providing a much-needed public service. The consequence of this is that services become trapped in a cycle of unrealistically low levels of funding, able each year to get only marginal increases to their grant when what is required is a nine- or tenfold increase.

There is also the problem of exploitation. The incidence of unemployment among disabled people is higher than the average (Office of Population Censuses and Surveys, 1988 and 1989). There is likely to be, therefore, a greater potential for recruiting disabled people as volunteers. But if those people would choose to be employed and to receive a wage or salary for their work, is it right to design services that exploit their willingness to volunteer because they cannot find paid work elsewhere?

Despite these reservations, it seems certain that volunteers will continue to play a significant role in the future provision of disability information and advice services. They should be selected with as much care as paid staff and they should be trained to equally high levels if they are to provide direct information and advice services. They should also be expected to work a minimum amount of time each week, for without that they will be unable to develop the skills and familiarity with the subjects on which they will be called to provide information and advice. The National Consumer Council

Standards do not draw a distinction between paid staff and volunteers. They do, however, note that:

> Advice work is, increasingly, a skilled occupation requiring the workers to build up considerable levels of practical expertise. To acquire such expertise will depend on the number of clients seen by each worker... Nevertheless it is recommended that all generalist advice workers, whether paid or unpaid, should work at least the equivalent of one full day a week (National Consumer Council, 1986).

The network of citizens advice bureaux has always relied heavily on the use of volunteers. Indeed it has been praised for its cost-effectiveness on these grounds. Yet it is useful to consider its experience. First it has acknowledged that volunteers make the most useful contribution when they are able to work within a clearly established framework. To establish such a framework usually calls for leadership by someone committed full-time to the service and to guarantee this it is necessary to create a full-time paid post. For some years all citizens advice bureaux have been required to have such a paid manager as a condition of membership of the National Association.

CAB workers are not allowed to offer direct advice services without first passing through a rigorous training programme that is compulsory for both paid staff and volunteers. Some bureaux that rely on large numbers of volunteers have found, however, that the training cost becomes very high. Linked to this is the high turnover in volunteers that some bureaux experience. Understandably they recruit volunteers who are able and who have at least the potential to develop a range of fairly high-level skills. A significant proportion of the volunteers see service in a citizens advice bureau as a step back into employment and, not surprisingly, take their newly acquired skills and experience onto the job market. Consequently, some bureaux spend a great deal of time and effort in recruiting and training volunteers who move into paid work after a short period.

The experience of the citizens advice bureaux service should lead all service providers to be cautious when establishing a service that is dependent on volunteer labour.

There is a general need for flexible working arrangements to accommodate any particular needs that disabled people may have, whether paid or unpaid. It should be possible to accommodate job-shares and part-time working and to enable people to work for only short periods if necessary. The services should also provide the equipment, facilities and technology necessary to enable people with particular impairments to work effectively. The need for such facilities should be self-evident, but it may be necessary to make the case when applying for funding.

Closely related to this is the need to make flexible arrangements to enable disabled people and carers to participate fully in management committee meetings. The timing of meetings can be critical and it may be necessary to make arrangements so that carers can attend meetings.

The NDIP experience

It is worth considering the staffing experience of the NDIP pilot projects. It should be borne in mind that these projects were relatively well-resourced and were able to offer reasonably good salaries and continuity of employment over a three year period. Yet despite this, a number of the projects found it difficult to recruit and to retain staff. It was also difficult to recruit staff who had the range of experience that we have identified in this chapter. The lack of skills and the lack of prior information and advice experience meant that a great deal of time was spent learning by trial and error.

Continuity of employment was very important, possibly because of the need to learn through trial and error. The Berkshire Disability Information Network was staffed in the early stages by a series of short-term contracts and these proved very unsatisfactory both for the development of the project and for the individuals concerned. The short-term contracts did not enable the staff to develop a thorough working knowledge of the project or to develop a sense of team-work. The project did not develop a momentum that could carry it through difficult periods and, as a consequence, progress was slow. Later the staffing arrangements were changed and staff were appointed on contracts that extended to the end of the project with the prospect of continuation if long-term funding could be obtained. There was a marked change in the rate of progress and in the quality of the developmental work that was undertaken.

It is dangerous to generalise from such a small base but, in other pilot projects, most was achieved in the projects that had the same staff throughout the three years of NDIP. The projects that were able to appoint early on and to retain the staff were able to build up a momentum and to make real progress. Others were not so fortunate, either because they had difficulties recruiting at the outset, or because they had to divert resources at critical times to recruiting and training new staff. In these cases progress was slower and more erratic. The projects were weakened by the loss of expertise and the need, in small workgroups, to re-establish working relationships.

The staff of a disability information and advice service are its greatest asset. They need to be selected with care, trained and developed and paid well. The service is too important to do otherwise. How, after all, would the average person feel if they consulted a lawyer or a financial adviser only to find they were dealing with an untrained volunteer who only worked for three hours once a fortnight?

References

Hasler, Frances (1993) 'The place of information provision in the disability movement' *In: Information enables: improving access to information services for disabled people.* Policy Studies Institute

National Consumer Council (1986) *Good advice for all: guidelines on standards for local advice services.*

Office of Population Censuses and Surveys (1988 and 1989) *Reports on disability* (Five reports). HMSO

16 Cheap, reliable and effective information systems

A considerable amount of progress has been made in the development of cheap, effective and reliable information systems for disability information and advice services. During the life of the National Disability Information Project new systems have been developed, tested and marketed. Local projects now have a range of different systems from which they can choose. There has been less progress at national level where developments have been held up through lack of resources. But even here, the prospects for future development are encouraging.

Experience at national level

At the time of the Coopers and Lybrand report there was a very positive attitude towards the use of information technology at the national level. Much of the enthusiasm emanated from a Technical Liaison Group that had been established by the Department of Trade and Industry to explore the contribution that information technology could make to the provision of disability information.

The Technical Liaison Group had undertaken a number of studies and was very optimistic about the use of large databases with dial-up online access (Insam and Millar, 1988). There appeared to be considerable support for the development of a national framework linking databases maintained by the national information providers. Disabled people or local information services could dial into this network and obtain the information they needed.

The Coopers and Lybrand report was cautious. They acknowledged the potential and recommended wider access to national databases such as that maintained by the Disabled Living Foundation. They noted that:

> It should be stressed, however, that under the present fragmented circumstances, proper access to this database would require a considerably higher number of terminals than would be the case were organisations federated (Coopers and Lybrand, 1988).

In fact the national information providers were a very long way from being able to take full advantage of the potential offered by the technology.

A number of factors inhibited development. First, and most significant, was the disparity in the level to which technology was being used by the national providers. One or two, notably the Disabled Living Foundation, had made a considerable progress in the development of technology. They had created databases containing their information and were using this to improve their service. The Disabled Living Foundation provided dial-up online access and was about to make the database available on CD-ROM. They were also exploring the use of interactive compact discs to provide a more sophisticated information product. In contrast, some of the other, smaller national providers were still struggling to come to terms with basic applications like word processing and were far from being able to exploit the potential of the technology. They were severely limited by the lack of trained staff and had insufficient resources to enable them to acquire up-to-date hardware and software.

There was also a problem of compatibility between systems. The Department of Trade and Industry had been promoting its Open Network concept and in the early 1990s there was considerable discussion of Open Systems Interconnection. Both developments were intended to improve compatibility and so facilitate the exchange of information between systems. But fully open systems were far from a common reality. The national information providers that had established databases had each invested a considerable amount of time and effort and were naturally reluctant to invest even more in re-formatting so that the information could be exchanged with other providers, or so that it could be accessed in a common way.

Even where electronic information services had been developed, the take-up was disappointingly low. The Disabled Living Foundation found it difficult to sell subscriptions to its database – DLF Data – and the service has taken longer than expected to become economically viable. This almost certainly is a reflection of the lack of resources in the overall system – an issue that was discussed in Chapter 12. The lack of take-up could also be a result of low levels of technology awareness among potential information users and a lack of the necessary equipment.

This lack of equipment has certainly inhibited the development of information products based on CD-ROM and interactive compact discs.

The other barrier to development was money. Each provider felt that they were operating at the limit of their resources and there was no additional money in prospect to underwrite the substantial development costs that would be involved.

In late 1992 representatives of the national information providers met to discuss what could be done collectively to exploit the potential of information technology. The view that emerged from the meeting was that, while individual providers would continue to make progress, there was relatively little that could be done collectively.

Future prospects

Information technology continues to offer considerable potential for national information providers. The technology itself is evolving all the time and offers increased capacity, lower costs and higher levels of sophistication. New products are being brought to the market and existing products are becoming better established.

Technological change will make it easier and cheaper to create information products and services that can better satisfy disabled people's information needs. It is, for example, possible to create, within acceptable cost limits, an interactive information product that will contain details of a wide range of aids and equipment, including video pictures showing how the equipment operates. It is also possible to produce cheap and robust interactive, hand-held systems that advisers can use on home visits to calculate benefit entitlements. Further possibilities are offered by the emerging networks like the Internet and CompuServe. These provide an opportunity to communicate and to disseminate information in an interactive format. They also provide opportunities for disabled people to participate in bulletin board services, exchanging information with one another. Developments such as these are likely to have a major impact on national disability information provision in the relatively near future. The technological problems are being overcome rapidly.

The information infrastructure is also being improved rapidly and is set for considerable extension in the future. The capacity of the tele-communications system is expanding and costs are coming down. Online access to remote databases will become both cheaper and more efficient in the future. At the same time, telecommunications-based information services like the Internet offer considerable possibilities for communicating information directly into the homes of disabled people, or at least, into the homes of disabled people who have both the familiarity with technology and the resources needed to exploit the familiarity.

Within Europe, the European Commission has invested heavily in the development of HANDYNET, a Union-wide information system for disabled people. This has yet to prove its worth and many people are sceptical of its immediate value. However, there are plans to develop a Common Information Area within Europe and such pan-European information services will become more and more common. The existence of HANDYNET will at least mean that disabled people have the basic framework of a service designed to meet their needs.

These opportunities can only be exploited by national information providers if other barriers are overcome. The current low levels of awareness of information technology certainly inhibit developments but levels of awareness and familiarity can change quickly if there is an incentive for them to do so. Only when more resources are introduced into the system will change come about. When disabled people can afford to access electronic information services; when all local disability information and advice services can afford to buy CD-ROM players or modems to link them to the Internet; when they can afford to invest in the necessary staff training. When all these changes come about, the market for electronic information services will flourish and the national information providers will be able to exploit the opportunities that are open to them.

Use at local level

One very positive feature of the National Disability Information Project was the fact that the 12 pilot projects were given relatively generous capital grants. All the projects purchased basic computers and printers and some were able to acquire equipment that enabled them to undertake relatively sophisticated activities like desk-top publishing.

The equipment was used intensively. All the projects used the three standard office applications – word processing, spreadsheets and databases. Word processing packages presented few problems and a number of the projects were able to extend their use into full desk-top publishing applications. A number of projects used spreadsheets as an aid to financial management and the Oldham Disability Alliance developed a fairly sophisticated project management system using spreadsheet software. Most of the projects set up databases to store and to manage local information.

These three basic applications have many obvious uses in local information and advice services and the NDIP pilot projects were able to demonstrate the contribution that technology can make towards improving office efficiency. The application that presented most problems was the development of local databases.

The database experience

In Chapter 12 we raised a number of questions about the creation of local databases and their role in information and advice services. Clearly, the need for a database, and the role it will play in the overall service, should determine the type of database to be constructed. In some services, like that provided by the Disability Information Service in Surrey (DISS), the database is used interactively by advisers when answering telephone enquiries. In other cases, like the Gateshead Disability Information Project, databases are used to store and manage information that is reproduced and used on paper in the form of directories or fact sheets.

In common with many other information and advice services, some of the NDIP pilot projects did not think carefully enough about the way in which the databases would be used before embarking on the process of creating them. Because of this, the guidelines on databases and directories give a strong emphasis to the need to integrate the database planning into the overall planning of the service (Rooney and Shiner, 1995).

By the end of NDIP, disability information and advice services could choose from a number of disability-related database packages that were on the market. This was not the case, however, when the pilot projects began operating and they faced a limited range of choices.

The Kent Information Federation established an arrangement with DISS whereby DISS mounted the Kent information on its database and made it available for use in Kent along with the national information on the database. In Devon the Disability Information and Advice Federation established a similar link with the county council, mounting its information on the council's mainframe database system to which the members then had access. This did, however, involve the creation of new software at quite considerable cost.

In all the other cases the projects developed their own databases, mostly using commercially available software. The nature and coverage of these databases varied considerably. The Birmingham Information Federation database contained information about the large number of members of the federation. In contrast, the databases established by other projects, such as the Berkshire Disability Information Network and GUIDE, were designed to contain information that could be used interactively as the basis for an information and advice service. Oldham Disability Alliance and the North East Yorkshire Information Service used databases to store and manage information that was then produced as an information pack or handbook for use by a range of professionals.

The experience of these projects was varied. In just about all cases, however, the database development took longer, was more complicated and was more expensive than anyone expected at the outset. This was the case whether the development was undertaken by the project staff alone or by technical experts brought in from outside. It is difficult to calculate the actual costs as these clearly varied from project to project and not all projects were able to keep sufficiently detailed records. The average cost of developing a relatively small database – about 1,000 records – was in the order of £40-£50,000 and the work required the equivalent of one person working full-time for about a year.

Even when complete, the databases were really only suitable for storing relatively simple, tightly structured information, such as the names, addresses and descriptions of local services. The databases were not able to handle complex, unstructured information, such as information about benefit entitlements in ways that made retrieval faster or more effective than from printed texts.

A greater range of choice is now available to disability information and advice services. Three types of system are available:

∘ Complete systems with software and information

• Shell systems ready to have data added

• Database development software

The complete systems with software and information are the most expensive but offer an attractive solution to a service that can ill-afford the investment needed to develop its own system. One of the NDIP projects has developed just such a system. In Gloucestershire the GUIDE service developed its own database using the CAIRS database management software. The database was made available to other outlets in Gloucestershire both through the health authority information network and as a stand-alone system. In 1993 GUIDE resolved to market the database and it is available in two formats. In can be purchased as a read-only database containing regularly-updated records of about 2,000 national organisations. Alternatively, local services can buy the national database with an added facility that enables them to enter their own local information. Similar packages are offered by Information in Cheshire (INCHES) and by DISS in Surrey.

These packages offer local services updated information on a range of national disability organisations; a range of different search methods including keyword and menu-driven searches; and the possibility of building local information into this framework. The systems are not, however, cheap. Costs in this area tend to change rapidly as the three suppliers compete with each other. At the time of writing the purchase price of the stand-alone systems varies from £600 to over £2,000. In addition, services need to pay an annual subscription to obtain the updated information. These subscriptions range from £200 to £700. The full systems range in price from nearly £1,500 to over £3,000 with, again, an annual subscription payable in addition.

The shell systems are much cheaper, ranging in price from £50 to £300. These provide a complete structure with templates for entering information along with menus and other facilities for searching for the data. The local service has to collect and enter the information into the system – this represents a large and fairly complex task if inconsistencies are to be avoided.

A system designed to meet the particular needs of disability information and advice services has been developed by the Computer Development Unit of the London Advice Services Alliance as part of their contract to provide technical support to the NDIP project. This is intended to provide a basic information storage and management system for local groups. Similar systems are available from Information for Action Ltd (Cata-LIST) and from Boston Information Technologies (Interlink). These have been developed for other voluntary sector groups and experience shows that a considerable amount of customisation can be required before they can be applied successfully in local disability information and advice services.

Most readily available are the database management software packages developed by international software companies like Lotus and Microsoft. These now frequently come as part of a software bundle which is pre-installed on personal computers. They offer a considerable degree of sophistication but require a commensurate level of skill to set them up and to customise the system to meet the particular needs of the local service. The magnitude and complexity of this task should not be underestimated.

To a great extent the information technology problems associated with databases are diminishing in significance. A number of different products are available from which local services can choose and it seems likely that in the future the quality, reliability and ease of use of these products will improve.

Information networks
Recent developments in telecommunications offer considerable opportunities for distributing and communicating information. In Devon, the Disability Information and Advice Federation provided information that was mounted on the local authority mainframe computer system. This meant that the federation database could be accessed in each social services office, public library and council building. To supplement the local information the county council subscribed to the Disabled Living Foundation's DLF data and made that available in the same way.

Other pilot projects mounted information on networks that were more directly targeted at members of the public. In Berkshire, the pilot project mounted information related to disability on BvS, the public videotex service. In Norfolk, the federation was contracted by the local authority to collect local disability information so that it could be mounted on the public videotex system maintained by the county council.

In Gateshead, the Disability Information Project was approached by the local cable television provider and, as a result, plans to provide a full range of disability-related information on an interactive videotex system available at no additional cost to all cable subscribers in Gateshead.

It was, however, in Manchester that information networks were exploited most fully. Manchester has developed, with support from the local authority and others, a sophisticated, public access electronic information network called the Manchester Host. Subscribers to the Host can use it to retrieve information from the various databases that are linked in. Or they can use the Host as a means of communication, sending electronic mail messages. It is also possible to mount bulletin boards on the Host and, in that way, to encourage the direct exchange of information between people with common interests. It is also possible to gain access to the Internet through the Host. Clearly, the Manchester Host offered considerable potential to the Manchester Disability Information Service (MDIS).

The original intention of MDIS was to use the Host to establish an information exchange for disabled people. The plan was to mount information on the Host and to encourage the development of bulletin boards and electronic mail. The information to be mounted was different from most of the other databases developed by NDIP pilot projects: rather than concentrating on the names and addresses of local organisations, the Host could be used to 'post' a wide range of documents – like the *NDIP Newsletter*, for example – that could be down-loaded by users onto their own computers. The advantage of this is apparent: if disabled people can down-load the documents onto their own computers, they can manipulate the text and generate an output that suits their particular needs. So the word processed electronic file containing the text of a newsletter could easily be sent to the HOST from where it could be down-loaded by a disabled person and output in large print, Braille or as synthesised speech.

Unfortunately, staffing problems and other factors limited the extent to which MDIS was able to exploit the Host. A considerable amount of information was made available on the system and it was used extensively as a communications medium by a relatively small number of people, but its full potential remains to be explored.

During the life of NDIP the Internet became established as a mass electronic medium. This offers, on an international scale, many of the possibilities that were being explored in the Manchester Host. And it is highly likely that the coming years will see a dramatic increase in the use of such networks by disabled people. As always, however, the limiting factor will be money.

Technology to overcome impairment

Information technology offers considerable potential for overcoming impairments, particularly sensory impairments. Kurzweil reading machines, for example, can scan printed text and 'translate' it into synthesised speech; personal computers can be linked up to Braille printers and a range of software is available to enable blind and partially sighted people to make full use of computers.

The adaptation of basic technology and the potential for manipulating information in electronic form offer real possibilities for disability information and advice services wishing to make information as accessible as possible.

The Gateshead Disability Information Project (GDIP) set out, as one of its two main aims, to explore the scope for using interactive compact discs to make information more accessible. Interactive compact discs were chosen because they were a technology aimed at the domestic market with the consequent likelihood both that prices would be low and levels of support and service would be high. The technology exploits the very high capacity of compact discs, and the ability to shift very rapidly from one part of the disc to another. The result is a package that presents information sequentially but which enables the user to interrupt, to go back and repeat information, to ask for more detail, or to skip sections. More particularly, interactive compact discs permit information to be displayed concurrently in different formats – sound, text and still or moving pictures.

GDIP investigated the potential for using this technology to make information more accessible for people with hearing impairments. They chose the CD-i system then being developed by Phillips as this seemed most likely to become established as a generally available domestic system.

They began by making a disc based on the RADAR publication *Into work*, a guide to employment for disabled people. The information contained in the booklet was re-presented on the disc in sound, pictures, sub-titles and in British Sign Language, using video pictures of a signer. Despite a number of technical problems the final product proved to be very successful (Gateshead Disability Information Project, 1993). The lessons learned from the first disc were incorporated in a second disc which provided a guide to hospitals in Gateshead. This presented the information in sound, sub-titles, British Sign Language and in the five minority ethnic languages that are used locally.

The Gateshead experience showed that the technology opens up new possibilities for the communication of information but that it is not always easy to exploit these possibilities. As the technology becomes more sophisticated, so it becomes necessary to develop ways of structuring and presenting information effectively. It reinforces the fact that it is not desirable simply to translate information from one medium into another. If the message is to be effective, the information must be designed so that it fits the requirements of the medium. This is an area of information design that is little understood. There is a pressing need for research and development to enable us to understand the different information design constraints and conventions of the different media.

Conclusion
The Gateshead experience with interactive compact discs, the Manchester experience with information networks and the range of database systems that are now available indicate both the progress that has been made over the last three years and potential for the future. As the technology becomes cheaper, more flexible and more sophisticated, there will be a continuing need to explore how it can be used to meet the information needs of disabled people.

References
Coopers and Lybrand (1988) *Information needs of disabled people, their carers and service providers: final report*. Department of Health and Social Security

Gateshead Disability Information Project (1993) *Into work: an evaluation report*

Insam, E and Millar, H (1988) *Access to databases for people with disabilities: network development studies 1: computer databases 1982-1987*. Department of Trade and Industry

Rooney, Michael and Shiner, Michael (1995) *Managing disability information: guidelines on directories and databases*. Policy Studies Institute

17   Development should not take place in isolation

Much would be lost if disability information and advice services developed in isolation. The information and advice services would lose the opportunity to benefit from experience gained elsewhere. Other service providers and groups of disabled people would not be able to gain from the specialist expertise of the disability advisers and information providers.

Through the National Disability Information Project we sought to develop links at national and local levels that would integrate disability information and advice services into the mainstream provision of advice services and into the wider disability movement.

Links with advice services

Disability information and advice services do not have a monopoly on information for disabled people. A disabled person with a housing problem, for example, is just as likely to seek help from a housing aid centre as they are from a disability advice service. Equally, large numbers of disabled people consult generalist advice services like citizens advice bureaux each year. It is important that all these services are accessible – in the widest sense – to disabled people. And the specialist information and advice services have a role to play in making the rest of the advice movement aware of their responsibilities to disabled people.

At one level there is a need to ensure that local advice centres are accessible by wheelchair users, and to insist that the local service providers make information available in formats that are usable by people with sensory impairments. These issues are, or at least should be, self-evident and the failure to make adequate provision is more often due to lack of resources than to lack of will or awareness.

More fundamentally, there is a need to ensure that all providers of information and advice are aware of the issues that affect disabled people. Only by being aware of the issues can information and advice providers begin to make the necessary provision. Specialist disability information and advice providers at both national and local level are in a good position to raise this kind of awareness. They come into direct contact with the issues and are able to build up specialist knowledge and expertise. Thus the National Association of Citizens Advice Bureaux might look to the Disability Alliance for specialist expertise on disability benefits; or a local education advice centre might look to the local DIAL group for advice on special educational needs provision.

The influence can operate at a number of different levels. The disability specialists may be able to help other services improve their provision for disabled people. Or it may be more appropriate to establish an understanding of respective areas of expertise so that clients can be referred from one service to another.

Local federations offer a mechanism for achieving this. They can provide a forum at which ideas and experience are exchanged. Or they can go further by providing support services and joint planning of services. It is, therefore, to be regretted that some federations are quite exclusive. Some restrict participation to disability information and advice services, some even exclude local disability information and advice services that do not share their particular aims or philosophy. In other cases – the Somerset federation is a good example – a wide range of groups is actively involved. These range from generalist advice services like the CABx, through statutory services like the local authority and the Benefits Agency, to disability information and advice services like DIALs and disability action groups. A membership as broad as this offers real opportunities for constructive dialogue and effective planning.

Most of the NDIP pilot projects sought to involve other providers of information and advice. The Berkshire Disability Information Network established some of its local information centres in citizens advice bureaux. In Norfolk, the federation established close links with advice services and sought to support them through the provision of training and specialist information. The Gateshead Disability Information Project was an active participant in FLAG – the Federation of Local Advice Groups in Gateshead. In Manchester and Birmingham, the projects established telephone-based referral services to direct disabled people to the most appropriate sources of help and advice, although in Birmingham people were only referred to services that were federation members. All the other projects referred clients to other local services.

At a national level there is reasonably effective liaison between the national information providers and other providers of information and advice. Two organisations in particular made efforts to develop stronger links. The National Association of Citizens Advice Bureaux (NACAB) committed its support at an early stage. It distributed the *NDIP Newsletter* to all its bureaux and contributed in various other ways – through participation in the national information provision working groups, for example. The Federation of Independent Advice Centres (FIAC) participated in a very similar way. In its case it was able to offer membership to the pilot projects and a number of them joined.

We also sought to establish a formal link through the Advice Services Alliance. This is an umbrella organisation that brings together the national networks of advice services: NACAB, FIAC, DIAL UK, the Law Centres Federation and so on. We were not in a position to apply for membership but we took steps to ensure that the members knew about the aims and activities of NDIP.

The Advice Services Alliance is very closely linked with the London Advice Service Alliance (LASA) which provides support services for advice services in Greater London. We entered into a contract with the Computer Development Unit of LASA to provide information technology support services for the pilot projects and with the Consultancy, Information and Policy Unit of LASA that provided administrative support for the national information provision working groups.

In these ways we sought to integrate the development of disability information and advice services into the mainstream activities of advice services. To a great extent, this was successful. At the outset, there was a good deal of antagonism towards NDIP within the advice world. The Coopers and Lybrand report had not been well received by many of the mainstream providers of advice services – a number of people thought that there had been a failure to take account of developments in advice services generally. Then there was a concern that there had been insufficient consultation immediately prior to the launch of NDIP. There were feelings that the project would simply reinvent wheels and that the resources could much better be employed in different ways. These attitudes have, to some extent, been justified. There is now, however, a degree of mutual trust that can provide the foundation for future cooperation.

Links with the disability movement

It is equally important for disability information and advice services to have close links with the disability movement. There is a substantial and growing number of local groups that represent the views and interests of disabled people. In some cases they provide direct services like accessible transport, in others they are mainly concerned with campaigning to improve the social, political and economic conditions of disabled people. Clearly, there are advantages to be gained if disability information and advice services link in with these representative groups. In North East Yorkshire, the NDIP pilot project worked very closely with three disability action groups and benefited considerably as a result.

Again there is a balance of benefits. The information and advice services benefit from the support and expertise within the disability movement, while the movement itself can benefit from experience generated in the information and advice services.

If information and advice services are to be effective, they should have strong links with the communities they serve. Just as housing advice services need to establish links with tenants groups, so disability information and advice services need to establish links with groups representing disabled people.

These links provide a means of keeping in touch with the concerns of disabled people. They also provide a means of tapping into the knowledge and advice that can only come from people who have experienced disability for themselves.

The disability movement also benefits. Effective information and advice services enable people to take more control of their lives. Instead of merely responding to the exigencies of a complex welfare state, people are able to exert influence, to exercise choice, to claim entitlements and to gain the wider benefits of citizenship. The circumstances in which many disabled people find themselves have traditionally meant that they find it more difficult to exercise their rights and to participate fully as citizens. Effective information and advice services can play an important role in redressing the balance.

In the future, this function will become even more critical. Disabled people are winning – or being awarded – more rights and more recognition. They will need information and advice if they are to be able to exercise their rights and to build on the recognition of their particular needs. As we saw in Chapter 2, the track record is not promising. Local authorities and others have statutory duties to provide services and to undertake action of various kinds that should benefit disabled people. Yet in many cases these duties have not be carried out and the action has not been taken – the employment quota is only one example. As the balance shifts away from placing duties on corporate bodies and moves towards the award of rights to individuals, so there open up greater possibilities for individuals to bring about change through the exercise of their rights. Information and advice services will have a key supporting role to play.

Information and advice services also have the potential to provide a powerful means of feedback to policy-makers. Through an analysis of the problems that are presented to them, it becomes possible to identify the critical areas of social policy and provision. The importance of this work lies in the fact that the feedback is based on direct experience of the difficulties that people have when dealing with legislation and the social welfare system. Information and advice services deal with the casualties of that system and are well placed to identify where changes are required. Because of this, many advice services have the provision of feedback to policy-makers as one of their main objectives. Organisations representing the interests of disabled people can clearly make use of this information in their lobbying and campaigning work.

Just as with the broader advice services, it has been possible to establish closer links with the disability movement during the life of NDIP. There was a degree of hostility at the outset. There was a perceived lack of consultation. There was a feeling that scarce resources were going to organisations outside the mainstream of the disability movement. There was also a concern about the fact that most of the pilot projects were controlled by people who were not disabled and the project team was similarly composed of people who had little experience of disability. Even some of the more established organisations *for* disabled people felt that the £3 million being spent on NDIP could be better spent within the established disability organisations.

These fears and concerns have, to an extent, been overcome. At local level most of the pilot projects have taken steps to ensure that disabled people are able to manage and control the services. More than half have adopted constitutions that ensure that disabled people are in the majority on management committees. They have also taken steps to recruit disabled people to staff the projects. This helps to develop and strengthen links with local groups of disabled people.

At a national level there has been less progress. The British Council of Organisations of Disabled People (BCODP) has not been able to endorse NDIP because it is not controlled by disabled people but there is no longer a sense of hostility. The research unit at Leeds University associated with BCODP was one of a number of research organisations invited to tender for an NDIP-funded study of the use of national information in local disability information and advice services (Barnes, 1994). And in various other ways other individuals associated with BCODP have contributed to NDIP activities through participation in local projects, by presenting papers at conferences and so on.

Other national organisations have provided a high level of support, particularly in connection with the NDIP work with national information providers.

National and local liaison

There is a need to ensure that there is effective liaison between information provision at national and local level. The overall provision of information and advice for disabled people calls for activity at both levels. The working groups that looked at the funding, pricing and quality of national disability information provision described an interrelated system with local services delivering information that has been collected and processed nationally. Such arrangements provide for economies of scale and the avoidance of duplication in the collection of information. They also ensure that information and advice can be delivered locally and tailored to meet the particular needs of the individual (Moore, Steele and Boswell, 1994).

There is still much to be done to improve the liaison between national and local information and advice providers. Colin Barnes found an unacceptable lack of awareness among local groups of what was available nationally (Barnes, 1994) and several national providers are only just becoming aware of the needs of local services and the contribution that they can make to delivering information to the people who need it. The directory of local disability information and advice services (Nadash, 1993) was made available in electronic form so that national information providers could add the information to their mailing lists and in that way promote their information to local groups. The annual national disability information conference also provides an opportunity for people from national and local levels to meet and to exchange information.

Local service planning

There is much to be gained from a planned approach to the development of local information and advice services. The services are generally small, financially insecure and are operated by hard-pressed staff. There is also, in most areas, a higher level of demand than can be met from existing resources. It makes sense, therefore, to plan carefully the way in which those resources are deployed. This has been acknowledged in a number of areas where local authorities have undertaken advice service planning exercises based on the National Consumer Council standards (National Consumer Council, 1986; Advice Services Alliance, 1987).

In many areas, there is a well-established network of information and advice services. Any organisation setting up a specialist service to meet the needs of disabled people needs to recognise this and to build on existing strengths rather than duplicating or competing.

It is in this area that the concept of federations of information and advice services is most valuable. The federations provide an opportunity for cooperation, collaboration and for joint planning. They provide a means whereby the providers of disability information and advice can interact with other advice services.

The federations provide a mechanism for taking things further and for providing common services, like training, or for sharing expertise. They also provide a channel of communication between the statutory and the voluntary sectors.

A number of the federations established as part of NDIP operated in this way but perhaps one of the best examples is provided by the Somerset Disability Information Federation which acts as a very effective forum for local information and advice services and which provides a bridge between the statutory and voluntary sectors.

National networks of local services

National networks perform a number of functions. They can provide services centrally where there are significant economies of scale. Such services include training, information provision, specialist consultancy and assistance with service development. Some networks have gone further and offer member groups access to indemnity insurance and pensions schemes. They provide a form of legitimisation for local services that have to conform to certain membership criteria.

The national network also provides a channel through which information and experience collected locally can be fed back to policy makers. In addition, the network can represent the interests of the local services in national forums.

A number of networks exist to perform these functions for local disability information and advice services. Some services are provided by local groups of national organisations like Age Concern, BCODP, MIND and Mencap and benefit from membership of that subject-focused network. There are, however, four national networks of disability information and advice services.

The largest is DIAL UK. This was established in 1977 when a group of local DIALs came together to form an organisation to represent their interests at national level. It now has 100 members and is supported by the Department of Health to provide an information service, training, service development and general support to its members. It also represents their interests at national level. A number of local DIAL groups were involved in NDIP pilot projects and DIAL UK has done much to support the overall development of NDIP.

The Federation of Independent Advice Centres (FIAC) was established at the same time as DIAL UK to bring together a disparate group of local neighbourhood advice services. It now has over 850 members, about 80 of which are disability information and advice services. It provides the normal range of services for its members and, in addition, has pioneered the provision of insurance and pensions schemes. FIAC has also supported NDIP, particularly through assistance with the working groups on national information provision.

An organisation was formed in 1989 to promote the concept of federations as providers of information and advice for disabled people. Originally called CHOICE, in 1993 it changed its name to the National Association of Disability Information and Advice Federations (NADIAF). This was always a looser association of interested individuals and organisations, rather than a national membership network. It organised a number of meetings and conferences but its activities were limited by lack of funds and the need to rely on services provided by individuals who had other pressing commitments. At the time of writing the future of NADIAF is unclear.

The Disabled Living Centres Council is the fourth network. It links together the disabled living centres, each of which provide information and advice as part of its basic service.

There is also the Consumer Health Information Consortium (CHIC) that represents local health information services. Many of these are based in the health service and have developed, or expanded, as a direct result of the *Patients charter* initiative that required health authorities to provide consumer information services. A number of disability information services are members of CHIC.

The other network that should be mentioned is the National Association of Citizens Advice Bureaux. Membership is only open to citizens advice bureaux and most specialist disability information and advice services are therefore ineligible on grounds of their specialist focus. However, a significant number of citizens advice bureaux offer specialist disability information and advice services. Some employ disability rights workers, others participate in the activities of local disability federations, while in Berkshire, the federation maintains information centres in a number of citizens advice bureaux in the county.

Conclusion

It is sometimes the case that national initiatives operate in isolation. This is particularly so when, like NDIP, the initiative involves local pilot or demonstration projects. Such projects can find themselves set apart from the mainstream of provision. They are intrinsically different from other provision being, usually, better funded and supported and attracting more publicity and interest that other services that might have been working away unrecognised for years. It is easy for the projects to be seen as cuckoos in an already crowded nest. To overcome this it is important to break through this isolation and to establish effective working links with developments elsewhere.

This was particularly important for NDIP. It was necessary to establish effective working links with established advice services, both locally and nationally. It was equally important to establish working links with the disability movement.

Initially the need to build these bridges was complicated by the hostility that NDIP, and the Coopers and Lybrand report before it, had engendered. Within the disability movement and the advice services sector, NDIP was not something to be welcomed, rather it was perceived as another example of government money being spent on a prestige and time-limited project while basic services were having to struggle to survive.

Three years later the climate is different. NDIP has now received the support of the advice services sector – many local advice services work closely with the pilot projects while nationally, the networks of advice services have done much to support and strengthen the overall initiative. Similarly with the disability movement. At both local and national level there is now a greater sense of cooperation and mutual support.

It is important to ensure that these effective working relationships endure beyond the life of NDIP. Real progress can only be made through working together, through the provision of mutual support and through the exchange of information and experience.

References

Advice Services Alliance (1987) *Going for advice: a manual for preparing local development plans for advice services*

Barnes, Colin (1994) *From national to local: an evaluation of the effectiveness of the national disablement information providers services to local disablement information providers.* British Council of Organisations of Disabled People

Moore, Nick, Steele, Jane and Boswell, Caroline (1994) *Improving the provision of national disability information.* Policy Studies Institute

Nadash, Pamela (1993) *Directory of local disability information providers.* Policy Studies Institute

National Consumer Council (1986) *Good advice for all: guidelines on standards for local advice services.*

18   An infrastructure to support further development

Even with goodwill and generous resources, there is a limit to what can be achieved in three years. The development of information and advice services for disabled people had been taking place for a number of years before the National Disability Information Project and, with luck, that process of development will continue long into the future. NDIP could provide a boost to that longer process – an injection of resources, enthusiasm and publicity – that would accelerate the pace of change and perhaps influence the direction to be taken. But it was always time-limited.

It was important, therefore, to help to establish an infrastructure that would support future development. Something that would remain after NDIP had come to an end. As the project drew to a close, we consulted as widely as possible to identify what was needed after NDIP in terms of a regional or national mechanism to further the aims and objectives established by NDIP. There was a remarkably strong consensus. The clear priority was the provision of support to establish and strengthen services at local level. To achieve this, people felt a need for a mechanism to enable them to exchange information and experience. They wanted a means of articulating their views at national level. They also wanted direct support to help them develop their services.

To realise these expectations, there was considerable support for the proposal to establish an umbrella organisation that would unite the various interested parties concerned with the provision of information and advice for disabled people.

Priority for local development
We saw in Chapter 11 that, when given a choice, people prefer to obtain information and advice in person from a service based in their local community. So, while national information providers have an important role to play in the overall system, much of the information and advice needs to be delivered at a local level. This calls for an effective network of

well-resourced, efficiently managed disability information and advice services.

The basic framework for that network exists. We were able to identify about 600 local disability information and advice services. Yet their effectiveness is limited. Many are new and are struggling to become established within their communities. On the whole, they appear to be poorly resourced, with many lacking sufficient funds to be able to deliver a complex and demanding service. There is a generally low level of experience in advice and information work and a very considerable need for training. In short, we are far from having the kind of network that can deliver effective information and advice services to all the disabled people who need them.

Through NDIP, a great deal has been learned about the operation of local information and advice services for disabled people. The experience gained through the 12 pilot projects and the contacts that were established with other local groups has meant that there is much that others can benefit from. Some of this experience has been codified in the guidelines that have been published during the project. Much more exists in the heads of the people who have worked on the projects.

The general view, as NDIP drew to a close, was that there was a pressing and continuing need for development and a basis for achieving it.

Exchange of information and experience

In any developing service there is a need for information about what is going on: about new forms of service that are being explored; about new information services or training opportunities; about changes in legislation or procedures. Without such information services develop in isolation and, almost always, offer a less-than-desirable level of service.

During NDIP this need was, to an extent, met through the *Newsletter* and the *Current awareness bulletin*. The *Newsletter*, in particular, made a considerable impact – the mailing list grew steadily during the project and for most of the project over 6,000 copies of each issue were distributed. The *Current awareness bulletin* was originally intended only for the 12 pilot projects, where it was widely distributed. In response to demand, the *Bulletin* was made generally available for the last two years of the project.

When faced with a problem in the development or management of a service, it is possible to learn a certain amount from published guidelines. In most cases, however, it is better to talk to someone who has successfully confronted the same problem. The national conferences provided opportunities to meet and to exchange this kind of experience.

There was strong support for the continuation of the *Newsletter,* the *Current awareness bulletin* and the conference to provide opportunities to exchange information and experience.

Direct support for service development

To support what can be learned through informal contacts, there was felt to be a need for direct support for the development of local services. This, it was felt, called for a person or an agency that could provide very practical help with things like the drafting of constitutions; the establishment of management committees; the selection and organisation of information sources; the installation of information systems; the preparation of grant applications and service proposals, and the establishment of office procedures and financial systems. Closely related to this was the need for training both in specialist skills and in the general management of voluntary sector organisations.

The aim should be to provide the support needed to help new services to become established and young services to mature.

A voice at national level

People felt that there was a need for a mechanism which the government and others could use to listen to, and take account of, the views of local services. In any parliamentary democracy, there is a continuous process of consultation and dialogue. The government needs to obtain views on its proposals and it needs to find out what are the consequences of past policies. Other organisations, whether pressure groups or service providers, need to articulate their desires and needs to government and to express opinions on what is, or is not, happening.

Many local disability information and advice services felt that they did not have the opportunity to participate in this exchange of views and opinions. Members of national networks like DIAL UK and FIAC were able to have their views expressed but others were not so fortunate. Even the DIAL UK and FIAC members felt that there was a danger that fragmentation would mean that any general message from the local services would not be delivered with sufficient weight.

There was also a need for a forum which would improve the communication between national information providers and the local services.

People felt, therefore, that there was a need for an overall organisation that would be able to represent the interests of all local disability information and advice service providers.

The Alliance of Disability Advice and Information Providers

In the summer of 1994 a number of organisations came together to discuss life after NDIP. The meeting was convened by DIAL UK and attended by several of the national information providers and by representatives of three of the NDIP pilot projects. There was general agreement that the priority should be the development of local services and the main tasks should be to provide opportunities to exchange information and experience; to provide direct support for local services; and to provide a voice for local services at national level.

Two strands of development emerged. The group decided to prepare for the establishment of an the Alliance of Disability Advice and Information Providers. The aim was to carry out some of the background work and to consult as widely as possible ready for discussion and a possible launch at the National Disability Information Conference in March 1995.

The proposal was for a membership organisation controlled by disabled people representing local information and advice services. It would provide the overall, uniting framework that could be seen to represent the views of local service providers. To carry out the preparatory work, 15 organisations agreed to a common set of aims and objectives and proceeded to formulate a draft constitutional framework.

Members of the Steering Group for the Alliance of Disability Advice and Information Providers

Advice Services Alliance
BCODP
Centre for Accessible Environments
Devon Disability Information and Advice Federation
DIAL UK
Disabled Living Centres Council
Disability Alliance
Disability Wales
Federation of Independent Advice Centres
Kent Information Federation
NACAB
NADIAF
National Information Forum
RADAR
Scope

The group also applied for funding under Section 64. The funds would enable to Alliance to continue the *Newsletter*, to run conferences and to employ staff who could provide the direct support for local groups.

At the time of writing the outcome of the Section 64 application is unknown, as is the reception that the proposal for the Alliance will receive at the March 1995 conference. What can be said, however, is that there was almost unanimous agreement that something should be done to maintain the momentum established by NDIP. And what has been achieved so far has been achieved harmoniously and in a spirit of very constructive cooperation.

Part IV

Was it all worth it?

The National Disability Information Project cost £3 million – £1 million a year over three years. Over that period the Department of Health could have made a dramatic increase in the Section 64 grants to the national information providers. Or they could have met in full the annual running costs of about 20 reasonably funded local disability advice services. Did they make the right choice?

Of course, the question is not a valid one. The resources that were made available for NDIP were only available for three years. The support needed by national and local services needs to be committed over a much longer period – short-term increases in funds can cause as many problems as they solve.

Also the intention was different. The essence of development projects like NDIP is the fact that they enable projects to experiment – to do things that might otherwise be hard to justify to permanent funders. They provide a means of accelerating the process of learning through trial and error. They permit new solutions to be tested and evaluated. Some solutions will be abandoned, others will be incorporated into mainstream provision and will, in future, be supported by the long-term funders. NDIP provided the opportunity to bring about change by learning through experience.

The questions that should be asked, therefore, are: how much have we learned? how much has changed? and did the Department get value for money?

Part IV – Contents

19 National information providers

The first aim of the National Disability Information Project was to improve the effectiveness of the national information providers and to promote greater coordination.

The first report from the evaluation team at the Research Institute for Consumer Affairs (RICA) considered the impact that NDIP had made on national information providers. It concluded that it was difficult to identify much significant progress (More O'Ferrall and others, 1993).

Effectiveness

The national information providers have not remained static during the three years of NDIP. They are all working to increase their effectiveness and to improve the services that they offer. And many have made considerable progress. NDIP, however, can claim little credit for this. Most of the impetus towards improvement has come from within the national information providers themselves.

That is not to say the NDIP has had no influence at all. In some respects the Project has been able to shape thinking and to improve matters.

An important step forward was the identification of the main national information providers. As we noted earlier in Chapter 8, a large number of organisations are concerned with the generation of information relevant to disabled people. By identifying the 29 main providers we focused attention on them and, through the directory (Hinkley and Steele, 1992), provided local services and others with the information they required to make full use of the services. The directory went further than simply listing the organisations. It identified and discussed the main issues that were, at that time, concerning the information providers and in this way provided the foundation for much of the work that followed.

NDIP also provided opportunities for the national information providers to exhibit their products and services to local information and advice services. In 1992 we organised an exhibition at PSI to which local disability information and advice services were invited and the National

Disability Information Conferences have provided further opportunities for the national providers to demonstrate their services. Through the directory and these exhibitions, NDIP has increased awareness of what the national providers can offer.

There is also a better appreciation of the relative roles of national and local information and advice services. Before NDIP there was, among some national information providers, a feeling that they had to meet all the information needs alone. A number had established telephone enquiry services and were finding it very difficult to allocate sufficient resources to staff such services adequately. Three years on, there is more of a sense of partnership and a willingness to work more closely with local services. This is due, in part at least, to the increased awareness of local disability information and advice services that has arisen through NDIP.

The two most concrete attempts to improve the effectiveness of national providers were the working groups on quality and on funding and pricing. These arose from the early discussion of common problems and they were an opportunity for representatives of interested providers to come together to share experience and to exchange ideas and views. The immediate response has been good. The results of the working groups have been well received (Moore, Steele and Boswell, 1994). It will, however, be some time before the full effect of the working groups can be assessed.

Coordination

It proved very difficult to bring about greater coordination. To an extent, the problem was one of unrealistic expectations. The aim of NDIP was 'to promote greater coordination' and written into the brief for the project team was a requirement to coordinate the work of the national information providers. Yet coordination is only possible if the person or organisation doing the coordinating has some control over those being coordinated. Coordination is not possible without the power to coerce or the willingness by others to be coordinated.

In the case of NDIP there was no power to coerce and only a limited willingness to be coordinated. All of the national information providers are autonomous organisations answerable to their own governing bodies. Quite rightly they defended their independence and their freedom to act as they choose. Each was willing to agree to coordination provided that it did not involve them doing anything that they would not do anyway. In adopting this approach they were not being unreasonable – they were simply reflecting their independence.

The matter was further complicated by the fact that the organisations varied widely in size, some employing only two or three staff, others being very much larger. They also differed significantly in the importance attached to the provision of information. In some organisations, providing information was a marginal activity while in others it was the primary function. This meant that staff of differing levels of seniority participated in the discussions. Some were in a position to commit their organisations to particular courses of action, others were not.

Money also created a barrier to coordination. Most of the national information providers are funded through Section 64 of the *Health Services and Public Health Act 1968* and to a great extent they compete for scarce resources. In such circumstances few organisations are prepared to relinquish their independence. The position was made worse during NDIP by the changes taking place in the Section 64 funding and by the very real concerns that such changes brought about.

Some representatives of the national information providers, in discussion with the evaluation team from RICA, felt that some of the NDIP funds should have been given to national information providers so that they could undertake project work. The fact that such funds were not made available did little to enhance the working relationship (More O'Ferrall, 1993).

The best that could be hoped for was to promote greater cooperation by adopting a joint approach towards the solution of common problems.

By identifying the 29 main organisations, NDIP provided a starting point for such cooperation and joint action. Before that there had been a number of *ad hoc* groupings of national providers, such as the Disability Information Coordination Committee, but these groups only ever represented a minority of the main providers. NDIP provided an opportunity for representatives of the main providers to meet and to identify common problems.

It is interesting to speculate on what the agenda might have contained had it been possible to coordinate the national providers. A number of topics were suggested for inclusion: common computing standards; the exchange of information; the elimination of duplication; and the use of a standard classification scheme. It is worth exploring each of these in a little more detail.

In the long run there is considerable potential for the adoption of common computing standards. This would make it easier for national information providers to exchange data and, in this way, avoid duplication in the collection of information. More particularly, it would make it easier for local services to access the databases of the national providers. But, as we saw in Chapter 16, the level of computing varies considerably between the national providers and, as things stand at present, all that could realistically be done would be to reduce matters to the lowest common denominator. This would seriously disadvantage the more advanced users of information technology. The alternative – to raise standards to something approaching the level achieved by the most advanced – would require a level of investment that is way beyond the bounds of reasonable expectation.

The technology itself is also changing and converging towards greater interchangeability, if not to common standards. Thus, we have reached a point where text produced in one word processing system can be read by most others and data in one spreadsheet format can be manipulated by most of the other packages on the market. Database packages are not yet quite so interchangeable but they are likely to be so fairly soon. These technological developments will steadily erode the need for the national providers to adopt common standards – they will soon be able to exchange information and communicate with each other even though they use different systems.

There are many benefits to be gained from the exchange of information: the duplication of effort in collecting the information can be reduced and the value of information services can be increased by the addition of information collected by other providers. But this pre-supposes voluntary cooperation between the providers. In fact, many of them compete with each other. And although the benefits of information exchange are greatest between providers working in the same or in closely related subject areas, this is precisely where the competition is greatest. The scope for increasing the exchange of information through coordination is, therefore, implicitly limited by the degree of competition that exists in the system.

The elimination of duplication is often held to be a considerable potential benefit. Yet, as the working group on funding and pricing showed, a system that has no duplication offers little choice to consumers. In fact, during the three years of NDIP we found no evidence to suggest that duplication was a problem or that it increased costs significantly. Indeed, there was some evidence to suggest that consumers would benefit from greater choice in the sources of information available to them.

The greatest potential lies in the use of a standard classification scheme for the information services and products. If all national information providers pre-classified their information according to an agreed classification scheme then local services would not have to classify the material themselves. This would result in a substantial saving of time across the system as a whole. Here some considerable progress was made during NDIP. The evaluation carried out by the University of Central England showed that the classification scheme developed by the Disability

Information Service in Surrey provided a sound basis for general use by local services (Nankivell, 1994). As this scheme becomes more widely used, national information providers will be able to add value to their information by pre-classifying it. It is, however, interesting to note that the pressure to identify a generally applicable classification scheme arose from the local services not from the national providers.

Conclusion

Our overall conclusion is that NDIP has done something to improve the effectiveness of national information providers, but the impact will not be fully apparent for some years. As for coordination, little has been achieved but, under the circumstances, that is not surprising.

NDIP has helped to raise awareness of disability information and to promote the role of the main national information providers. Set against the prevailing concerns about resources under the changed Section 64 arrangements, however, the impact has been marginal.

References

Hinkley, Philipa and Steele, Jane (1992) *National disability information provision: sources and issues*. Policy Studies Institute

Moore, Nick, Steele, Jane and Boswell, Caroline (1994) *Improving the provision of national disability information*. Policy Studies Institute

Nankivell, Clare (1994) *Can the DISS classification scheme be developed for national use?* University of Central England

More O'Ferrall and others (1993) *Evaluation of the National Disability Information Project: interim report and summary of work in progress*. RICA

20   Local disability information and advice services

Locally, the aim of NDIP was to encourage the development of effective local information and advice services. In this there have been many more identifiable achievements.

The balance of funding within NDIP was tilted heavily towards the local services – more than 95 per cent of the Project's resources were directed, in one way or another, towards developments at local level. The twelve pilot projects provided opportunities to test new ways of organising services and to stimulate development elsewhere.

Many of the pilot projects did more than experiment with new ways of delivering services. They actively tried to help development elsewhere. They did this in a number of ways – by producing publications, training manuals, computer packages and videos and by working with other disability information and advice services to pass on their experience and to help establish new services.

One concrete measure of achievement is the fact that about 600 local services exist to provide information and advice services to disabled people in England. We do not know for sure whether the number of services increased during the life of NDIP as we only surveyed them once but the clear impression that we formed through contact with them was that many had come into being since the announcement of NDIP in 1991.

It is more difficult to assess whether or not the effectiveness of those local agencies improved as a result of NDIP.

Effectiveness
The biggest problem facing most local disability information and advice services is a lack of resources. We have seen in Chapters 9 and 14 that many, if not most, local services operate on a level of resources that is well below what is required for a fully effective service. Until that basic problem has been overcome, the effectiveness of local services will always be constrained.

There is some evidence to suggest that NDIP has helped local services in their arguments for the resources they require. First, the publicity given to the launch of NDIP and the subsequent publicity that the Project and the local pilot services have received has contributed to a general raising in the level of awareness of the need for disability information and advice services. Local services have been able to use the existence of NDIP to legitimise their applications for funds.

The project team sought to build on this by producing guidelines on fundraising for local services (Shiner, 1993). These have been well received and should have helped local projects in their efforts to secure funds.

Within the limits set by the level of resources available, the effectiveness of a local information and advice service depends on a number of factors: the quality of the staff; the management of the service; the relevance of the service to the needs of the community; the quality of the information and the information systems in use; and the relationships with other local services. NDIP has contributed to improvements in most of these areas.

The project team have not been able to do much to help local services improve the quality of staff. Had more time and resources been available, more could have been done to investigate the training needs and skill requirements of staff working in disability information and advice services. We could have built on this to develop training courses or learning packages that could be widely used. This is, however, one area that should be high on the list of priorities for any organisation that succeeds NDIP.

Effective management of services was one thing that was emphasised throughout NDIP. The pilot projects learned a great deal about the development of constitutions; the organisation of management committees; and the steps needed to ensure that services were controlled by disabled people. This experience has been passed on through the *Newsletter* and through extensive discussions at conferences and other meetings. In a more concrete way we produced a set of guidelines on planning and evaluating local services (Simpkins, 1993). It has to be recognised, however, that this was the area where most time was spent reinventing wheels. Many of the organisational and management problems faced by the pilot projects were common throughout the voluntary sector. For the pilot projects the difficulties were compounded by the federation concept with its requirement for multi-agency working. But essentially, the staff and management committees of the pilot projects were climbing a learning curve that had been climbed by many others.

No matter how efficient a service is, it can only be effective if it is meeting the needs of the community it serves. A number of the pilot projects invested considerable time and effort in research into the information needs of disabled people. Not all of this work was as productive as it might have been. To help others with this difficult task we produced another set of guidelines (Simpkins, 1994).

NDIP has contributed directly to the development of improved information and information systems for use by local services. One pilot project – GUIDE in Gloucester – has marketed its information; an information system to manage it; and a thesaurus of terms that can be used by local services. The Computer Development Unit of the London Advice Services Alliance has also developed, with NDIP support, an information management system aimed specifically at local disability information and advice services. Through NDIP the DISS classification scheme was evaluated and the researchers concluded that it could form the basis for a generally applicable scheme. We also sought to disseminate the experience of the pilot projects in establishing databases and directories (Rooney and Shiner, 1995). There have, therefore, been a number of concrete developments that should improve the effectiveness of local services.

It is likely that NDIP has also had an indirect effect. During the three years a number of other systems and services have become available. DISS now offers both information and an information management system and there is a range of other services, as we noted in Chapter 16. The existence of NDIP helped to provide a framework within which it became viable to launch such services and products.

The project team also sought to promote cooperation between local services. At the most basic level, we encouraged local providers of disability information and advice to work together and to share experience. We also tried to extend that spirit of cooperation to other local advice services, to other parts of the disability movement and to local service providers. This approach to cooperative, joint working has been a characteristic of NDIP from the outset. In part is has been a direct consequence of the federation approach to service delivery. At a national level, we have sought to create a framework for local cooperation by working closely with national networks of local services.

One particular issue needs to be considered: did the pilot project develop and test new forms of service delivery? The answer here is fairly negative. The extent of innovation was limited. Some pilot projects did test things that were genuinely innovative. Gateshead, with its interactive compact disc, is probably the best example, along with Devon with its training video. In general, however, few of the services or activities undertaken by the pilots can be described as innovative.

It is, however, necessary to qualify that statement. Much of what was done was new to the groups that were doing it, and in some cases, previously untried in that locality. But many of the databases, directories, approaches to quality assurance, schemes of accreditation, and forms of service delivery were commonplace elsewhere. This is not so much a reflection on the 12 pilot projects, rather it is a consequence of the selection procedure that identified them.

It seems reasonable to conclude, therefore, that NDIP has contributed to an improvement in the overall effectiveness of local disability information and advice services. More particularly, the impact of NDIP will continue through the guidelines, the publications and other products produced by the pilot projects and the commercially available products and services that have come into being over the last three years.

The federation approach

It is not possible to conclude without assessing the viability of the federation approach that was advocated by the Coopers and Lybrand report and that formed the basis for the initial call for proposals under NDIP.

The Coopers and Lybrand report (1988) recommended that all information providers in a locality should come together:

> To provide a coordinated approach to information provision and to improve accessibility and quality of services. Such a federation should include statutory and voluntary agencies as well as groups of people with disabilities.

The report went on to identify the following key tasks for a federation:

- To set up effective liaison machinery between appropriate agencies.

- To identify gaps in provision and to develop strategies for bridging them.

- To manage and steer the development and implementation of local systems.

- To provide signposts for disabled people, carers and service providers.

- To ensure that services are monitored and evaluated for effectiveness.

- To ensure that services are consumer-led.

In the subsequent report by PE International a number of organisational structures were put forward (these are discussed in some detail in Chapter 9). It is easy to become sidetracked by questions about the viability of these organisational structures. What is more important, however is the answer to two more fundamental questions: is the federation approach feasible in the sense that it is the most effective way of achieving the tasks listed above? and does it deliver better services for disabled people?

Feasibility and effectiveness

A number of the NDIP projects actively sought to make the federation concept work. They adopted an agenda of tasks that was very similar to that set out above.

The pilot projects in Berkshire, Devon, Gateshead, Kent, Norfolk and Oldham took on most of the Coopers and Lybrand tasks and they have carried them out successfully. A number of factors appear to have contributed to their success.

First, each of the projects received strong support from the statutory sector. In some this came in the form of financial support, in other cases it was moral support and assistance with management or administrative matters.

Secondly, each project benefited from strong personalities and leadership. The importance of this element is not to be underestimated. Information and advice services are labour-intensive activities where the quality of the service offered depends greatly on the staff providing it. Strong personalities and leadership are vital.

Thirdly, the projects were founded on an existing pattern of services or were able to work with a well-established network of services. In short, they had something that they could federate and coordinate. Even here, the picture varied considerably. In Devon, the federation as such existed prior to NDIP. In Kent, the federation had either to create the satellites or to persuade existing organisations to join the federation. In Berkshire there was a range of agencies that were suitable hosts for the local information centres, although it was necessary to invest considerable amounts of time and effort in establishing the local federations.

Finally they were able to benefit from two factors that are crucial to the success of any development project: clear objectives and continuity of staffing. Clear objectives are essential. If everyone concerned does not know what a project is trying to achieve, time will be wasted and resources will not be used to greatest effect. In two of this group of projects there was an early period when objectives were unclear and progress was held up. Once the objectives had been agreed, however, development proceeded briskly. Similarly, the progress in one project was initially constrained by the lack of staffing continuity that arose from a series of short-term appointments. Once staff on longer-term contracts were appointed the rate of progress accelerated markedly. Equally important is the continuity of staffing. Changing staff can be very disruptive. Time is lost and inevitable delays result from the fact that a new staff member requires time to settle into a new job. The disruption caused by staff turnover or by the inability to appoint staff with the required skills and ability can significantly inhibit the development of a service.

It has to be recognised, however, that the organisational structures adopted by these pilot projects were not radically different from those that are commonly found in the voluntary sector. Certainly, the projects in Gateshead, Norfolk and Oldham were structured in a typically voluntary sector way. They were autonomous bodies governed by a management committee formed from representatives of the statutory sector and local groups in the community. Berkshire, Devon and Kent were different in the sense that they had a federal structure with satellite branches, or local federations that exercised some degree of influence, over the central unit.

Alongside these projects that were able to achieve the Coopers and Lybrand objectives must be set another group which were not able to do so. Birmingham, Manchester, North-East Yorkshire and Walsall all tried to follow the Coopers and Lybrand agenda but, for a variety of reasons, were unable to do so.

Again there were a number of contributory factors. In some cases geographical factors inhibited development. In North East Yorkshire, for example, differences in the characteristics of the three areas within North East Yorkshire were so significant that it proved impossible to develop an integrated service. More concrete progress was made following the decision to split the project into three separate entities.

In other cases there were a range of institutional conflicts that got in the way of effective development. Related to this was lukewarm support from the statutory sector. Both these issues contributed to organisational, constitutional and management problems. In Walsall these problems very severely inhibited the development of the service.

All four of the projects – in Birmingham, Manchester, North East Yorkshire and Walsall – also demonstrated the importance of strong leadership, clear objectives and continuity of staffing.

The project in Gloucester – GUIDE – did not conform to the Coopers and Lybrand model of a federation. Here the project was based on an information service provided by the health authority. Joint working with the voluntary sector, initially at least, mainly consisted of the involvement of some voluntary sector bodies in a steering group that in practice is better described as an advisory or consultative group. While this arrangement meant that the Coopers and Lybrand tasks were not really appropriate, it did have other benefits. The objectives of the service were very clear and there were few, if any, opportunities for institutional conflict. The project benefited from both continuity of staffing and from strong leadership and, as a result, achieved a much of what it set out to do, although it failed to make significant progress with the development of services to people with learning disabilities. Its efforts were, however, mainly concentrated on its own service and on information outlets in the health sector.

Two other projects did not attempt to follow the Coopers and Lybrand agenda. The element of the Gateshead project that was concerned with the development of interactive compact discs was clearly separate. As was the project in Southwark. This had started off following the Coopers and Lybrand agenda but after a year it was decided to re-model the project and to concentrate on two research themes, both of which were successfully pursued.

The conclusion from this appears to be that the federation model can be made to work successfully under certain circumstances but it is by no means universally applicable, nor is it sufficiently robust to withstand some of the problems that are endemic in the voluntary sector. The agenda of tasks set out by Coopers and Lybrand and by PE International is non-contentious. Achieving those tasks in any circumstances would do much to improve the quality of service, whether it be the provision of information and advice services for disabled people, employment counselling for the long-term unemployed or day nurseries for pre-school children. The tasks are a prospectus for the effective development of community-based services in the voluntary sector.

The problems arise in the organisational structure advocated by Coopers and Lybrand and PE International. In particular, multi-agency working has not been shown to be an effective way of working. There are some examples where joint arrangements worked very well: the collaboration between Gateshead Council on Disability and the Gateshead MBC Libraries and Arts Service, or the supportive relationship between the Devon federation and Devon County Council both show what can be achieved. In other pilots, however, multi-agency working fostered conflicts of interest, confusion of objectives, tussles for power and control and seriously muddled the distinction between purchaser and provider.

There is little evidence to suggest that multi-agency working delivers effective services any better than the more traditional arrangement of an autonomous organisation managed within the voluntary sector by an elected or representative management committee but independent of the statutory sector.

The test lies in the following question: was the success of Berkshire, Devon, Gateshead and Kent attributable to the federation structure, or would it have happened under a more traditional organisational structure? The answer lies in the factors that contributed to the success: personality, trust, mutual support and adequate resources. None of these were dependent on the federation structure. In that sense, the projects can be said to have succeeded despite being federations, rather than because of it.

Better services for disabled people?

It is just as difficult to conclude that federations make a significant impact on the level of advice services for disabled people. We are faced here with a more fundamental flaw in the thinking underlying the Coopers and Lybrand report and the subsequent actions that have followed it. The federation concept is based on a misunderstanding of what people need from information and advice services. To that extent, the pilot projects had the dice loaded against them before they even started.

We were able to show in Chapter 12 that people facing difficulties both want and need access to vigorous, local advice services. The provision of information alone is insufficient. Advice services depend for their existence on skilled workers who are easily accessible and who can be consulted in person. The priority for development, therefore, should be to ensure that, within any locality, there are properly staffed disability advice services that disabled people can use, and that generalist advice services are accessible, in all senses, to disabled people. Instead, the emphasis in the Coopers and Lybrand approach is to try to ensure that information flows more efficiently through the system.

We should not, however, write off federations entirely. We need to ask whether they have, in fact, stimulated the development of the services that are actually needed. Have federations meant that there are more advice workers in action? Or, are those that existed already better able to do their work?

The answers to these questions suggest that federations have succeeded in some places better than in others. In Berkshire, for example, it has been possible to stimulate the improvement of the services provided for disabled people through agencies such as the citizens advice bureaux service but even here the emphasis is still firmly on information rather than advice. In Kent, the federation has played a very active role in the creation of disability information services in different parts of the county. In Devon the federation has done much to improve the quality of service provided through both specialist and generalist agencies. In Gloucester, where, as we have noted, they specifically exclude advice provision from their remit, the availability of the GUIDE service, and in particular its database, has helped to stimulate the development of specific information services, even though, as we have noted, GUIDE cannot be described as a federation in the Coopers and Lybrand sense.

In these and other cases, the federations have done little to stimulate *advice* provision for disabled people, even though they made have done a great deal to stimulate the provision of *information.*

One crucial question has to be asked: if the money that was spent on the pilot projects had been spent directly on the provision of disability advice workers, would the benefit have been greater? In all but two cases the answer is probably 'yes'.

In Devon, the project worker did much to improve the quality of information and advice provision by existing workers. Effort was put into improving training, quality assurance, information provision and monitoring and evaluation. The service received by disabled people has almost certainly improved as a result.

In Kent, the central team has stimulated the creation of an emerging network of services of information and advice services. It has helped them to become established and has provided direct support in the form of information materials and training. The number of disability advice workers operating in the county has increased significantly as a direct result.

In other cases the balance of benefits would probably have been greater if the money had been used to employ disability advice workers directly. We must, however, recognise that the purpose of NDIP was not simply to provide additional funds for disability information and advice services over a three-year period. Rather, it was an attempt to explore and to experiment with some novel forms of service provision. If the conclusion of this experimentation is that the most pressing priority is to increase the number of active disability advice workers and to improve their quality, then much will have been gained. Not least, funders will have a better understanding of where to direct their resources.

Conclusion

There may be a role for a central body to provide services to support the work of local advice agencies – both generalist and specialist – through the provision of training, information consultancy and representation at tribunals. But this presupposes the existence of an established network of services that can benefit from such support. We are far from that position in most areas.

In other words, the development of a federation seems to work best when the impetus comes from the bottom up: when a group of services come together to share resources and to carry out collectively tasks that would be beyond their individual capacity. Only in the case of the Kent federation was it possible for development to take place from the top down and even here they were at pains to stimulate development from the bottom up.

This also raises questions about economies of scale. The provision of training, information, consultancy and representation are all activities which require a certain scale before they become viable.

Our conclusion is that federations are far from being a widely applicable solution. They offer, at best, limited opportunities for improving the provision of information and advice services for disabled people.

Future provision should focus on the development of a vigorous, well-funded network of information and advice services that focus on meeting the needs of disabled people. Along with that should go a continuous effort to ensure that the services provided by generalist information and advice agencies are fully accessible by disabled people.

If the local services perceive there to be a value in coming together to benefit from scale economies, to exchange ideas, to undertake joint service planning, or to provide common services, then they should be encouraged to do so. But the impetus should come from the bottom up.

References

Coopers and Lybrand (1988) *Information needs of disabled people, their carers and service providers: final report.* Department of Health and Social Security

Rooney, Michael and Shiner, Michael (1995) *Managing disability information: guidelines on directories and databases.* Policy Studies Institute

Shiner, Michael (1993) *Fundraising: sources and skills for disability information services.* Policy Studies Institute

Simpkins, Rebecca (1993) *Planning and evaluating disability information services.* Policy Studies Institute

Simpkins, Rebecca (1994) *Researching disability information needs.* Policy Studies Institute

21 Was it all worth it?

The answer to the question 'was it all worth it?' is a qualified 'yes'. Qualified in a number of ways.

Qualified first by the fact that the answer is given from within NDIP itself. The members of the project team have been involved with NDIP for over three years. We have put a considerable amount of time and effort into making the project a success and we are very aware of how much others have contributed as well. So we start from a position where we want to be positive. After all, if we do not think it was worth it, then what hope is there for any of us?

A more objective answer will be provided by the RICA evaluation team.

Our positive response is also qualified by an acute awareness of what could have been achieved if things had been done differently or if we – the project team and the pilot projects – had anticipated problems better. Hindsight is a wonderful thing and almost certainly it is possible to look back on even the most successful projects and see where improvements could have been made.

The success of NDIP was qualified in a number of other ways. The project was, for example, constrained by time. There was relatively little time to submit the initial bids. Once accepted there was great pressure to get projects up and running, to appoint staff, to acquire premises, to set up systems and to begin spending the money before the end of the financial year. Then, after what seemed like a relatively brief period of stability, we were approaching the end of the project. Three years seems a long time, but that time can slip away very quickly particularly in a project troubled by staff turnover or by other changes that disrupt the timetable.

The project was also constrained, particularly in the early period, by the criteria established for the selection of the pilot projects. The requirement to involve both the statutory and the voluntary sectors, for example, created a set of potential and real obstacles to the successful development of local projects. Also, the emphasis on information, as distinct from advice, failed to reflect the most pressing needs experienced by the people that NDIP set out to serve.

Another constraint was the project team's inability to coordinate the autonomous national information providers. This, and the looming uncertainty within the Section 64 system, inevitably meant that, nationally, we were unable to achieve as much as was expected of us.

The final qualification stems from the fact that it is simply too soon to tell what the impact of NDIP will be. It will have failed if all it has managed to do is to bring about some short-term improvements to the provision of information and advice for disabled people. It can only be said to have been successful if it has triggered and supported a process of long-term change and development that will lead to a steady improvement in the extent and quality of services.

These qualifications aside, it is possible to draw some conclusions.

First, the experience gained during NDIP has made it clear that there is a significant need for effective information and advice services to enable disabled people to cope better with the problems that society presents them. Such services should be vigorous and partisan in favour of the users. They should be controlled by disabled people; they should be located in the voluntary sector and they should be funded adequately by local authorities, possibly with support from health authorities. These local services should be supported by efficient and high-quality national information providers that are themselves responsive to the needs of users. This national provision of information should receive financial support from government.

Within that broad framework, we can go a little further and say that, while cooperation, the exchange of information and joint working are all desirable objectives, the concept of federations as set out in the Coopers and Lybrand report does not represent the most cost-effective way of meeting the need for disability information and advice.

NDIP has undoubtedly helped to clarify those issues and as such, it has been valuable. If that was all that had been achieved, however, it would have been an expensive use of £3 million.

The greater value lies in the stimulation that NDIP has given to the broader development of disability information and advice services. These services would have developed without NDIP. What the project has done is to give that process of development a boost. Through the publicity that NDIP has attracted; through the efforts that have been made to place disability information and advice on national and local agendas; through the opportunities that have been created to enable people from all kinds of services to exchange ideas and experience; and through the building of bridges with the wider disability movement and the rest of the advice services sector, NDIP has been able to stimulate and accelerate the creation of a network of services that will improve the quality of disabled people's lives.

To the extent that NDIP can be said to have achieved this, it was worth it.